Francis Ferguson Jr
20th Feb/74

CASTING OUT THE EVIL SPIRITS.

TABLE TIPPING.

THE RAPPERS:

OR,

THE MYSTERIES, FALLACIES, AND ABSURDITIES OF SPIRIT-RAPPING, TABLE-TIPPING, AND ENTRANCEMENT.

BY

A SEARCHER AFTER TRUTH.

NEW-YORK:
H. LONG & BROTHER,
121 NASSAU-STREET.

TO

The People of the United States

THIS WORK

IS RESPECTFULLY DEDICATED,

WITH THE EARNEST HOPE THAT IT WILL FORM A MITE TOWARDS DESTROYING A DELUSION WHICH IS DAILY WORKING EVIL AMONG THOUSANDS.

CONTENTS.

BOOK I.

A CIRCLE OF VISITS AMONG THE RAPPERS.

PREFACE.

In presenting to the public this volume on the subject of "Modern Spiritualism," as it is called, the author has only a few words to say. He made the series of visits among the "Rappers," comprised in Book I, with the single purpose of seeing and testing the nature of the "wonderful spirit manifestations" alleged to proceed from tables and entranced persons, and he has written down faithfully and truly all that he saw and heard. He has purposely mingled some pleasantry in his descriptions, but has never suffered that pleasantry to falsify a single word or manifestation alleged to have been uttered or exhibited by a spirit. As the table tipped, or as the raps came, he has described it, and as the alphabet or the entranced medium spoke, he has given it word for word. If the whole appears absurd on the face of it, and the alleged spirits look like very poor imitations, it is not the author's fault; but it must be charged to the account of the tables, the raps, and the entrancements—must be ascribed in fact to some other and very different causes than voices from the spirit world. The main part of the second book of this volume, is a compilation of the various philosophical theories which have been broached by others, in explanation of the "spiritual phenomena," and this compilation, together with the author's visit among the "Rappers," and the contrast which he has drawn between the "religion of Rappers and the religion of Christ," will, he trusts, present the subject in a complete and satisfactory light before the reader.

BOOK I.

A CIRCLE OF VISITS AMONG THE RAPPERS.

THE RAPPERS.

CHAPTER I.

THE BELIEVERS AND THEIR BELIEF.

In the city of New York, to which circle our personal investigation has been confined, there are, at the least calculation, forty thousand sincere believers in Spiritual Rappings. We cannot pretend to give the number of the disciples of this new Spiritual doctrine, scattered throughout other parts of the United States. It is sufficient to say, that it is immense, and far greater than the public generally imagine. These believers are to be found in every class of society from the highest to the lowest, and among minds of every degree of capacity and cultivation, from the most accomplished scholar down to the most ignorant of the ignorant. The rush to consult the spirits, both in what are called public and private circles, is so great, that, could New York be unroofed, either in the day or at night, a spectacle of Spirit Rapping would be exhibited, which would astound the public by the magnitude of its extent and almost ceaseless continuance. From morning until noon, from noon until night, and from night until morning again, in parlors where flashing mirrors reflect rosewood, and velvet, and silver, and gold; in humble rooms where the floors and walls are bare, the tables are placed, and around them, men and women, with their hands spread out, and eyes fixed as if on vacancy, are seated, waiting for communications from the Spirit World.

And your true believer in Spiritual Rappings is a man to be noted and marked wherever he goes: Spiritual Rapping with him is a religion not put off and on at intervals; he is no Sunday professor of his belief, but an every day worker in it, sitting motionless alone in the solitude of his own room, going to private circles where he can get admittance, and spending his money freely at public ones—seeking and asking only for raps and communications from the spirits of the other world. And from morning until night, and from night until morning, whether he is at the circle, or sitting alone, or in his bed, or at work, he is expecting these raps and communications; he is expecting to hear the spirits rap on tables, and from thence receive messages from them; he expects to hear them tap on his bedpost, to feel them grasp, or jostle, or knock him in the street, in his store or shop, in his room—at all times and in all places, he is confidently expecting at any moment to be subject to direct spiritual influence—the world's material substances and the bodies of mankind also are, to him, but so many objects for the spirits of the other world to knock upon and thus communicate with mortals. Of such believers as above described, there are, as we said before, not less than forty thousand in the city of New York. We have, during our investigations, seen a number of this description—seen them in circles and in private, conversed with them, and read the spiritual communications which they say, and sincerely believe, they have received. And we have seen such believers not only in the persons of young and credulous men and maidens, but in the persons of men and women where gray hairs and hard wrinkles had set the seal of age and incredulity; and in all, the devotion was complete and the faith boundless. Such being the believers, let us turn to a brief synopsis of their belief.

The disciples of the Spiritual Rappings believe that, on the death of the body, the spirit passes into another world, the position of which, in the sphere of worlds, or the particular nature of which, they do not pretend to describe. They say that it is not Heaven, neither is it Hell; it is not midway between the two, and it is not a place where God can be seen. They say it is rather a school of progress, where the spirit, when it first becomes a real spirit, that is, when it is freed from the body, goes to learn and advance higher and higher, until it reaches perfection. They believe that this spirit world has seven spheres, and each sphere seven circles; they believe also that the world of mortals has its spheres and circles, and that in both this world and in the spirit world, the spirit of man occupies a higher or a lower sphere, according to its capability and purity. They believe that when a man dies his spirit passes into that sphere of the spirit world corresponding the nearest to the sphere which he left in this world. They, therefore, as a natural consequence, believe that the spirit world is a most heterogenous place, full of good spirits and bad ones, highly developed and very ignorant ones—all, however, mixing together, knowing of each others' movements—some quite miserable, some supremely happy, and others in a medium state—but all advancing, learning and growing better, through the successive circles and spheres, until they shall go beyond the seventh. At this seventh sphere, the Spiritual Rapping believers pause: they profess, as far as we are now informed, no knowledge of the spirits beyond the seventh sphere of progress, as there has been no communication from the spirits on the subject.

This latter point leads us to the belief of the Spiritual Rappers on the subject of the communication between this world and that of the spirits. They believe that the inhabitants of the Spirit World are ever wandering about this; that not only the spirits of a man's dead relatives and friends are around him, or at least ready to answer his call, but that any other spirit is ready to answer him, and communicate with him; nay, even volunteer to do so, even at the time when he is seeking a communication from the spirit of one whom he knew on this earth. They believe also that some spirits of the Spirit World, who are not very highly developed, that is, not much better than they were when they left the earth, will lie to, abuse and trifle with, those of this world when they are in the act of seeking spiritual communications. Even good spirits, when holding communication with mortals, will often joke. The Spiritual Rapping disciples believe that communication with the Spirit World can only be had through the intervention of what is called a Medium; that is, some particular mortal to whom either the spirits take a fancy, or who is spiritual enough for them to hold direct intercourse with. Many are Mediums without knowing it, but it is supposed that sooner or later they will find it out. The Mediums place their hands on a table, in connection with those who seek communication, and the table tips, or raps are heard on it or under it, and thus the spirits testify their presence and willingness to be interrogated. Three raps or taps mean "yes;" one, "no;" and two, "I don't know," or "doubtful." When the spirit speaks by raps, the answer, if it be a name or place, or date, an alphabet constructed by the Mediums spells out the meaning. Often, however, the spirit communicates by taking possession, according to the belief of the Spiritual Rapping disciples, of the Medium, and compelling him to write what the spirit would say. So much for Spiritual Rapping belief.

There are, according to this Spiritual theory, six kinds of Mediums, viz:

Rapping Mediums, being those persons through whom the supposed spirits manifest themselves by sounds on the table or other places.

Tipping Mediums, being those persons through whom the supposed spirits manifest themselves by tipping tables, &c.

Speaking Mediums, being those whom the supposed spirits throw into a state of entrancement, and then speak through them.

Singing Mediums are those through whom the supposed spirits sing by means of entrancement.

Writing Mediums, being those of whose hands the supposed spirits take possession, and compel them to write as they, the spirits, dictate.

Impressible Mediums, being those whom the supposed spirits impress to think as they, the spirits, wish.

THE CIRCLE.

The first Spiritual Rapping Circles to which we shall take the reader, were public ones. The visitor to the public circles pays a small admission fee, the philosophy being, that the Mediums, although in daily communication with the Spiritual World, have not yet arrived at that degree of spirituality which will enable them to live without food and clothing; that they are still mortals and must work, like all mortals, for money.

In the early part of an evening, we rung the bell of a fine three-story house, and were ushered into the presence of Mrs. B., a public Rapping Medium. We expressed our desire to be introduced, if possible, to the spirits, and were accordingly invited to join the circle which was just at that moment forming. We entered a room, neatly furnished, and found some fourteen persons, male and female, seated around two tables, one of them covered with a green cloth, the other bare. The party, this evening, being rather too large for the usual table employed, the second one, which was a common ironing-table, had been, on the spur of the moment, pressed in from the service of the kitchen to the service of the spirits. Before Mrs. B. took her seat to preside over the circle, and while she was absent for a moment in another room, a respectable old gentleman very solemnly placed his hands on the table and suggested that probably, if the rest of the company followed his example, they would get a communication without the help of Mrs. B., intimating at the same time, that he believed he was something of a medium himself. The circle placed their hands as the old gentleman wished, but the spirits were as silent as the grave.

Mrs. B. now appeared. She is a fine-looking woman, portly in person and bearing, with jet-black hair, and an intellectual expression of countenance. She was richly dressed, and bore in her hand a gold watch, to which was appended a massive gold chain. The watch was to time—not the spirits—but each mortal in the Circle; for each mortal in Rapping Circles is often apt to talk so long to the spirits, that he interferes with the rest of his brother seekers after spiritual knowledge. Mrs. B. having taken her seat at the centre of the two tables, all hands were spread, and the performance or ceremony commenced.

First Gentleman—"Is there any spirit here wishing to communicate with me?"

Three raps ("yes,") loud and distinct, under the table.

A curious observer, in a large overcoat, here peered under and around the table, but the feet were all quiet, and the prospect, so far as any explanation of the manner in which the raps were produced was concerned, was a perfect blank.

First Gentleman here wrote inquiries on a paper, which he kept concealed; and the answers to them, made by the raps, which were now again resumed, were declared by the gentleman to be wrong.

Second Gentleman—Called up a musical spirit, and asked him to rap a tune. Hail Columbia was rapped, first in slow measure and then in quick, and excellently well rapped in both.

Third Questioner—Was a lady, dressed in mourning, young and interesting in appearance, with a high, pale forehead, and a bright speaking eye. She asked if her little daughter was present.

Three raps answered that she was, and would make her mother a communication sometime during the evening.

"Have you been with me, little daughter, all day, and did you come here with me?"

Three raps "yes."

"Are your guardian spirits with you?"

One rap "no."

It seems, according to the Spiritual Rapping belief, that the spirits in the other world have also their guardian angels.

"Do you know how many came here with me?"

"Yes."

"Can you name them?"

"No."

The little spirit, however, did afterwards (so the questioner said) name two of them correctly.

Fourth Questioner—A gentleman, who asked for the spirit of his father and mother. The answer was the mingled rapping of two distinct rappers, and the gentleman not being able to make out either, gave the matter up, and expressed himself satisfied—how, he did not say.

Fifth Questioner—Called up the spirit of his father, who, when asked what was his age when he died, gave answer that it was fifty years, which was five years beyond the correct answer. One of the circle here remarked that the spirits in the other world kept no account of time, that time was only kept in this world and that one spirit had answered him that he (the spirit) had been so happy in the Spirit World, that he had forgotten all about his age and life in this.

This was all of any consequence that was done at Mrs. B.'s circle, while we were there present. The spirits, it was remarked, did not appear on that night to be very communicative, and we accordingly left. Previous, however, to our leaving, it was stated by some of the circle that several nights previously a remarkable Spiritual manifestation had taken place in that room. A highly respectable physician of New York, with his wife, was present, and wore gaiters over his shoes; each gaiter was fastened with twelve buttons; and, while the physician was seated at the table, another member of the circle present asked a spirit to unfasten the doctor's gaiter and hand it to another gentleman present. Before the doctor knew anything about it, the gaiter was unfastened and handed as directed.

The next Spiritualist whom we visited was Mr. C., a public Tipping Medium. He is a young man, pleasing in his manners, slight in person and complexion. We found three gentlemen at his circle, and some four or five others, both ladies and gentlemen, just on the point of leaving. Mr. C.'s room was plainly furnished, with a common black walnut table in the centre, covered with slips of paper and lead pencils.

First Questioner—"Is there any spirit present who wishes to communicate with me?"

Three tips of the table, "yes."

"Who is it?"

Mr. C. here told the questioner to write the names of four or five living persons, and of one dead, on separate slips of paper, double them up so that no one could see them, and then throw them on the centre of the table. This was done by the questioner, who wrote on the slip of the dead the name of his brother.

"Now," said Mr. C., "we will take each paper and ask the spirit present to pick out the slip on which is written the name of the dead friend or relative of whom you (the questioner) are at this moment thinking."

Mr. C. did so, and when he held up the wad of paper on which the questioner had written the name of his dead brother, the table tipped three times, to signify that that was the one.

The arm of Mr. C. at this moment seemed to be seized with a violent spasm; he caught hold of a pencil and wrote away with a spasmodic rapidity, that to the observer appeared as if a streak of lightning was erratically amusing itself with tracing pot-hooks and hangers.

First Questioner—"Mr. C., what is the matter—you seem to be writing under some slight excitement?"

"The spirit has possession of me, and I *must* write whatever it dictates. I have a communication for you."

And, by the time he had thus answered, he ceased writing, and read to the questioner the following communication from his mother:—

My Dear Son—I am happy that you are willing to receive truth, and the happy hour that reunites mother and son will be looked forward to with pleasure.

(Signed,) A.

Questioner—"Can my mother spell me out her name?"

One tap of the table, "no."

Several names, and among them the name of the mother, were then written by the questioner on slips of paper, and doubled up as before, so that no one but himself could see or know their contents. The spirit, at the right name, tapped three times, as much as to say, that is the right one.

The same questioner was now answered by the spirit of his brother, whose name he had before written, and told correctly the name of the place where he died, which was spelt out by alphabet. The spirit also, after having answered several other questions without making a mistake, again invisibly took possession of Mr. C.'s arm, and sent the following communication to the questioner:

Dear Brother—You ask for evidence. Spirits cannot answer all questions, as their friends desire. For my part, I am happy that I can control this medium's hands, to convey my thoughts on paper. I want you to give a careful investigation to this subject, and be slow to receive; digest nothing which does not harmonize with your reason.

This communication was signed with correct initials of the questioner's brother's name. So the questioner acknowledged in the presence of the circle.

To the question of which sphere he was in, the brother answered that he was in the fourth, and he sent the following communication:

Dear Brother— Death is different from what I supposed it to be. It is only the waking up, as it were, from a long dream. In whatever stage of progress the spirit was when in the body, that sphere it enters in the Spirit World. Cultivate your spiritual faculties, and never heed the dogmas of the day.

Questioner—"I want a just idea of God."

(Spelt out by alphabet.) "I do too."

"Is there a personal God?"

"I believe I shall see a personal God, but never have; the spirits do not see God."

"Is there a personal devil?"

"No: the idea of a personal devil is a humbug."

Second Questioner (to Mr. C.)—"May I ask some mental questions?"

"Yes."

And the questioner, after writing some questions on a paper, remained silent for some time, during which the table at intervals tipped the answers yes and no. The questioner having finished, he was asked if he had received correct answers. He answered by reading the following question, as one which he had put:

"Was it spiritual agency that caused the ship Great Republic to be burnt?"

The answer to the question was "Yes."

This questioner did not favor the circle with any more of his questions or answers, and we are therefore not able to give the nature of either.

The above was all of any note that occurred while we were at Mr. C.'s circle, and we left with our budget of spiritual information. The reader will observe that in writing this chapter, we have adopted the language of the Spiritualists, and said the *spirit* says so and so. We do not mean by this to assert that it was really a spirit who answered the questions and made the communications; we mean only to say that it was the voice of the raps on, and the tips of the table, as interpreted by the mediums, and we have only used the word spirit for convenience. Our own ideas on the matter we shall give at the proper time. Meanwhile we are on a tour of investigation, and the above is our first instalment of facts, of which we have personal knowledge.

CHAPTER II.

THE TRAVELLING SPIRIT.

Our third visit was to the rooms of Mrs. C., a public Rapping Medium. The apartment in which Mrs. C. called up the spirits, or rather in which the spirits were called up, through the medium of her presence, was a large, well furnished one, having a round table in the centre, covered with cloth. Mrs. C. is a woman of slight and delicate, but well-formed figure, with small and regularly chiseled features, complexion clear and white, auburn hair, and eyes large, blue and expressive. She is, in her appearance, decidedly *spiritual*—just such a looking person as one would suppose the spirits, if in reality they do select any mortals for their favorites, would be likely to choose as the medium of their communications to this world. Mrs. C. informed us, that it is now nearly five years since she first discovered that she was a medium, and the discovery was made in this wise. A lady asked her to sit up at the table, when a spirit present informed her, to her astonishment, that she was a medium. During the first year afterwards, the spiritual manifestations to her were by indefinite sounds of various kinds, which accompanied and were heard around her, wherever she might be. Since then, she has become a regular medium, and the spirits not only rap, in general at her request or the request of others when she is present, but they take possession of her, and through her hand write communications.

It was evening when we visited Mrs. C., and the circle was very full, some fourteen or fifteen being around the table. The most marked individual in the group was an elderly gentleman, with hair as white as snow, forehead finely developed, and features giving evidence of great energy and decision of character. This gentleman had a sheet of paper before him, and was, as we entered, busily engaged in writing down his questions to the spirits, and their answers. There was a profound silence in the room, as the questions which the elderly gentleman put were entirely mental, and therefore known by none of the company but himself. His eyes, as he put the questions, were intently bent on the paper before him, with an expression which seemed to say, that while his ear was open to catch the faintest rap or sound, his soul was also open and waiting to receive some test, if he could possibly get one, of the presence of a spirit which should convince him that it was in reality a spirit with whom he was holding communication. The elderly gentleman, metaphorically speaking, had evidently taken off his coat to the spiritual business before him, and had determined to find out something if he could.

In the deep silence of the room, the raps in answer to the elderly gentleman's mental questions, were clear and distinct, and given with great promptness. Sometimes the questioner, however, would be in doubt whether the taps were two or three, and he would then in a sonorous voice say, "Will the spirit repeat that answer and rap the answer distinctly?" and the answer would be three loud raps given in quick succession and with great energy, as if the spirit intended that its "yes" should be emphatic.

Suddenly the raps, which had been continuous, ceased altogether, and the elderly gentleman with his pencil was brought to a stand still. He looked up from the paper in amazement, and repeated his question, but there was no response.

Mrs. C.—Perhaps there is a spirit present that will communicate with some of the other gentlemen, and it would be well, therefore, for the circle to pass the question around.

A young lawyer of New York, whose profound legal ability and estimable social qualities are universally acknowledged, but whose faith in Spirit Rappings is somewhat less extensive than the Russian Empire, even without the addition of Turkey, here took up the questioning of the spirits rendered vacant by the cessation of the spiritual communications to the elderly gentleman.

Lawyer.—Will any one talk with me?

The table gave forth no sound in answer, not even the faintest intimation of a rap was heard, and the lawyer was nonplussed as he continued in a slightly elevated voice and somewhat of a professional tone, "Won't you come and answer?" But the table was silent as before; the witness refused to appear, and as there was no competent judge present to compel attendance, the lawyer gave it up, and leaning back in his chair, looked at the gentleman next in order in the circle, with that legal resignation of countenance, which is always in court understood to say to the opposite counsel "The witness is yours, sir."

Before, however, the next gentleman took up the question, Mrs. C. suggested to the lawyer that he had not asked the spirits in exactly the right form, and perhaps if he would put the question in the usual manner, as—"Is there any spirit present that will communicate with me?" he would get an answer. A smile illumined the countenance of the young lawyer as he complied with the medium's suggestion, but the spirits remained silent as before, and the young lawyer had no rap or raps.

The question, "Is there any spirit present that will communicate with me?" was now asked in succession by all in the circle, Mrs. C. included, but the lawyer's fortune attended the whole, and the spirits appeared to have taken their departure entirely.

Various opinions in regard to the unaccountable absence of all the spirits, and the abrupt departure of the one which had been communicating with the elderly gentleman, were expressed by several persons at the table. Mrs. C. herself remarked it was an unusual circumstance, while one gentleman suggested that possibly the spirits were keeping New Year.

All remarks, however, on the movements of the spirits were suddenly checked by a nervous motion on the part of the arm of Mrs. C., and all eyes were immediately fixed on her, in order to see what result the nervous motion would produce.

" A spirit wishes to write a communication to some one here, and we shall soon see who it is," said Mrs. C., seizing a pencil and piece of paper, which latter article seemed involuntarily to fly towards the elderly gentleman who had been asking the mental questions, which the spirit had so suddenly ceased answering, leaving the whole circle in silence.

" It is for you, sir," said Mrs. C., " and possibly we shall now see the cause of the abrupt departure of the spirit with whom you were communicating," and Mrs. C.'s hand wrote with the rapidity of a race horse, and with a series of jerks far outrivalling those of an omnibus sleigh over the crossings of the streets at the last end of sleighing.

The spirits having finished jerking the arm of Mrs. C., and her pencil having performed its work, the manuscript was exhibited, and it was found to be written not only backwards but bottom upwards. None of the visitors present, of course, were linguists enough to decipher such writing, although it was handed round the table and subjected to the closest scrutiny. We ourselves examined it, and it appeared to us very much like what a telegraphic dispatch, announcing the destruction of the tower of Babel, would have been in that day of the confusion of tongues, supposing that the

Babelites had advanced so far in knowledge as to possess a lightning express in good working order. But the communication of the spirit, although an unknown language to all the rest around her, was simple English to Mrs. C., and holding it up to the elderly gentleman, she read as follows:

Dear Brother—I have been to see and he will retain it. (Signed) Eliza.

The communication, although now read in plain English, was still Greek to all around with the exception (as it appeared from his looks) of the elderly gentleman. He sat for a moment with his head leaning on his hands, his eyes fixed with an intense gaze on the table before him, and his whole manner betokening deep thought. Seeing, at length, the looks of curiosity around him, he raised his head and said to this effect:

"This is astonishing, and I will now tell the company the questions which I have mentally asked, and written down on the paper before me as I have asked them, and the answers to them. I first asked the spirit which said it was conversing with me, (the gentleman did not name the spirit,) if it was the same spirit with whom I had conversed a week ago, and it answered "yes." I had asked this spirit, a week ago, in another circle, within what time a certain event took place, and it announced three weeks. I this evening asked the same spirit the same question, and it answered four weeks, which makes the answer as correct now as it was a week ago. The next question I asked was of the spirit of my mother. I asked her if she would tell me about a gentleman in North Carolina, and whether he would retain a certain thing. The spirit answered "no," and then, gentlemen, as you all know, the raps on the table ceased, and neither you or I could get any communication until Mrs. C.'s arm was seized, and the communication of my sister Eliza was written to me as you have seen. She took the mission which my mother refused, and her going to North Carolina to gain the information I desired, accounts for the stillness at the table, and my inability to get any more raps while she was gone. These questions of mine have been test ones, and I consider that I have had proof of spiritual agency in the matter. No one at this table but myself knew or could know the questions I asked, and yet you see yourselves, the marvelous answer I have received."

The elderly gentleman having thus opened his budget to the whole company, and explained the perfect propriety of his sister Eliza's answer, which was before incomprehensible, and the company themselves having seen the communication signed "Eliza" by Mrs. C., and learned that the elderly gentleman had in truth a sister by that name—all this being developed before the persons present at Mrs. C.'s table, there was, of course, a variety of expressions in the faces of all. Some looked astonished, others looked blank, one or two smiled, and the young lawyer with a solemn face asked, if there was yet any spirit which would communicate with him. But the spirits again repudiated the law in the person of its young representative, who again leaned back in his chair and left the same question to go round the whole circle with the same success, except in the case of one quiet little man to whom a spirit professed its willingness to communicate. But the quiet little man had no questions to ask; said "he'd rather not," and there was silence again in the circle.

The silence was broken by the elderly gentleman, who asked if the spirit of his sister Eliza was still present, and on being answered in the affirmative, asked if the spirit of Mary Jane was present. The answer was "Yes."

"Will she communicate with me?"

"No."

"Will you write out the reason why?"

"Yes."

Mrs. C.'s arm was again seized, and a second tower of Babel dispatch writing was the result. The writing being interpreted, was as follows:

Dear Brother—Mary Jane will not communicate because she is not progressed far enough.

The elderly gentleman again expressed himself satisfied, saying that the answer was appropriate, as Mary Jane was but an infant when she died.

The next questioner, who was so fortunate as to hold communication with a spirit, asked of the spirit of his sister the name of the person who came into the room with him. After writing down a number of names on a slip of paper and pointing to each one in succession, the spirit indicated by raps the name of the right one.

This spirit also rapped out correctly her own name, the name of the place where she died, the names of her children living and the places where they now live. The questioner told the writer of this that every question was true to a hair.

The spirits after this appeared to have entirely departed, for no one at the table could get the smallest possible rap. The circle, therefore, broke up, and taking the arm of our friend, the young lawyer, we issued into the street, where living spirits were slipping upon the sidewalk most ungracefully.

"What do you think of it?" said we.

"Humbug," was the young lawyer's answer.

We neither assented or dissented, for we were on a tour of investigation, and our opinions were under lock and key until we had finished our investigations.

With our young friend the lawyer, we adjourned to the rooms of another medium, but was not fortunate enough to find him in. After we separated from our friend, we proceeded homeward. We asked mentally as we passed along the street, and even when we arrived home and were snugly ensconced in bed, that the spirits would give us some strong manifestation of their presence with us, by grasping us, rapping on our bed-post, or doing anything which would astonish us; but there was no answer, and we dropped off into a sweet sleep, undisturbed by any manifestations, but watched over, we hope, by a guardian angel, who will, we trust, keep us straight in all things.

CHAPTER III.

TWO YOUNG GIRL MEDIUMS.

Our fourth visit was to a private circle at the house of a Mr. T., to which we had been invited by that gentleman. A friend, with small faith but immense whiskers, accompanied us. The house, at the door of which we rung, was a plain two story wooden one, and evidently the residence of those in the middle walks of life. We were received by a lady of tall and commanding figure and intelligent countenance, who introduced us immediately into the room where the circle, she informed us, had been already formed. We found the room, which was not large, but furnished with the most scrupulous neatness, full of people. In the corner was a large circular table, on which rested a large bible, and around which some fifteen persons, both male and female, were gathered, with their hands spread out before them. The remainder of the company surrounded the circle at the table, in close phalanx, some standing, some sitting, and all evidently anxiously waiting some manifestation of the spirits. There was a dead silence in the room as we entered, and we ourself, together with our friend with the whiskers, endeavored to break the stillness as little as possible, in order that the spirits, if there were any present, should not have cause to say that we drove them off by our noise or abruptness. Mr. T., the gentleman of the house, politely offered us his seat at the table, which we accepted, and our friend in the whiskers having noiselessly, but with his eyes somewhat expanded, taken his seat close behind us, we had an opportunity to look more closely around us.

The members of the circle, in the midst of which we were seated, were persons respectable in appearance, plainly but neatly dressed, and evidently those who were no strangers to daily honest labor. The devout looks of many showed that sincere believers were plenty at the circle, while some shades of incredulity, which we detected on the faces of others, especially on that of a middle-aged gentleman with a very high peaked forehead, told us that unbelievers and curious inquirers were also present. Directly opposite us sat an elderly lady, with one of the neatest of caps bordering a face mild and benevolent in its expression, but so distinctly marked with firmness of belief as to be remarked by the most casual observer. She informed us at a later period of the evening, that she was a medium.

Seated at our left hand and next adjoining us, were two girls, the one fifteen the other sixteen years of age. The first was short and stout in person, with black hair and eyes, the bloom of the rose on her cheek, and her whole manner and expression of countenance artless and unsophisticated. The arm that was extended towards the table was full and round, and apparently of considerable muscular strength, while the hands, which were spread out on the table, although small and well formed, were evidently hands accustomed to the broom and brush. Mr. T. informed us that she was as she appeared, artless, possessed only of a plain education, and accustomed to daily labor, but that she was and had for some time been a medium, through whom the spirits spoke and sang, to whom they sometimes revealed themselves in palpable shape and form. The second girl was slight in figure, with light hair and eyes, pale complexion, artless in look and manner as her neighbor, and evidently of the same class and with about the same amount of education. She also was, as Mr. T. informed us, a medium of the same kind as the other.

The silence which reigned in the room for some time after we were seated was at length broken by sundry manifestations of impatience on the part of some of the circle, especially by the middle aged gentleman with the peaked forehead, the twinkle of whose large piercing eyes seemed to say as plainly as words, "I don't exactly know what to make out of all this, but if the spirits are coming I wish they would come."

The middle-aged gentleman with the peaked forehead however, did not content himself with looks; he spoke, and in a sonorous tone asked if there was any spirit present which would communicate with him. Hereupon, the elderly lady with the mild face, slapped her hand vigorously on the table, ejaculating at the same time "No." He of the peaked forehead looked at the lady, we looked, and our friend in the rear, with the whiskers, also looked, and we all looked inquiringly, but the elderly lady with her mouth firmly compressed, preserved the silence into which she had fallen immediately after speaking her emphatic "No." We hereupon took it upon ourself to speak.

Ourself—"Madam, how does your slapping on the table mean 'no?' We have been told that one invisible rap (supposed to be that of a spirit) on the table means 'no,' and when a person cannot see who raps, nor tell how the rap is produced, the rap then seems to be and mean something, inasmuch as it appears to be given by no mortal hand. But any one may rap on the table as you have done; and, as a test, the rap amounts to nothing."

Elderly Lady—"The spirit took possession of my hand, and I must rap as it directs."

Various persons in the circle now expressed themselves to the effect that they wished that the spirits would come in some shape or other. The usual question of "is there any spirit present who will communicate with me?" was passed round the circle, and the Mediums asked the spirits to tip or rap on the table. But there was no response, and the table remained still and firm on its legs. The elderly lady here suggested that if we would not make quite so much noise, the spirits would probably manifest themselves. The suggestion was heeded, and deep silence reigned in the circle. At this moment our friend in the whiskers, with his eyes more expansive than ever, touched us on the shoulder, and told us to look at the girl Medium with the light hair. Our eyes were already fixed in that direction. The girl's figure seemed to be intensely contorted. She bent her arms and twisted her body into all manner of shapes, the muscles of her face moved convulsively and her eyes rolled wildly. This was succeeded by her striking in quick succession her hand up and down on the edge of the table, not only with all natural strength, but apparently superhuman force, which seemed every moment as if it would result in a terrible laceration of the flesh and breaking of the bones of the hand. We ourself were shocked, and reached forth our hand to endeavor to stop the upward and downward strokes of the girl's arm, which rose and fell with almost the rapidity and thumping force of the beam of a steam engine. Our interference, however, was of about as much avail as if we had attempted to stop a locomotive, and so we gave it up, turning from the unpleasant sight and endeavoring to recover ourself somewhat by a contemplative survey of the incomparable whiskers of our friend in the rear. Our friend's eyes were dilated to their utmost capacity, seemed fairly to crack and snap, and to be just on the point of jumping beyond the line of his whiskers on to the girl. As we turned towards our friend, our looks evidently bearing witness to those around that we did not much relish the looking at the young girl thus apparently bruise herself, the elderly lady Medium quietly remarked, that the girl would not hurt herself, for the spirit which had taken possession of her "would see to that." We of course had nothing to answer to such a clincher, and after we had taken the short survey of our friend's eyes and whiskers, we again turned back too look more composedly on the young Medium. The strokes of the arm became less frequent, the face settled into a more composed state, and casting up her eyes, the girl said in a slow, distinct voice, but very different from the one in which we had before heard her speak, "Not one ray of hope." The spell seemed now suddenly to leave her, and giving a slight shrug to her whole frame, her face assumed its natural expression, and she took her seat with an air of slight embarrassment.

Ourself.—"Have you hurt yourself?"

"No."

"Do you remember anything you have been saying or doing?"

"No, only a little numbedness when the spirit first took possession of me."

At this moment, the girl Medium with the dark hair, who sat immediately next to us, was seized in like manner as the other had been. Her hands at first began to tremble, then her whole frame; her eyes rolled fearfully, and her arms became rigid as bars of iron. We tried with all our force, but could not bend her arms. This was followed by terrible writhings of her whole body, and a throwing out her arms in every direction as if she was in the act of resisting desperately some unseen power. She also struck her hands as violently as the other had done on the table. Finally, as before, the spasm, if we may so call it, became less violent, and a spirit (so supposed by the believers in this faith) spoke through her as follows:

"She would resist me, but she cannot. She made up her mind that she would not be influenced by the spirits. Some say that the departed are not allowed to return, but they do return to communicate with their friends. There is such a thing as progression, but not a devil.—There is no fire and brimstone. Spirits can progress. My name is Sarah. Adieu, my friends." Sarah was the medium's cousin.

After thus speaking, the medium shook herself, and came out of the trance as the others had done. Mr. T. informed us that this medium had been a speaking one and had spoken only in his circle, for about a year past. During the time that she was in the above trance, she reached forth and clutched the Bible convulsively, extending it towards one outside of the circle. The person took the Bible, commenced reading, and continued to do so until the Medium spoke as above. This led us to ask the question, if the spirits taught the religion of the Bible. The elderly lady Medium answered that such was her belief, and of many others.

At this moment the First Medium was again taken possession of by the spirit, but not in so violent a manner as before. Her face wore a smile, and her eyes were uprolled with a soft and blissful expression, as if she was contemplating some sight of beauty. Waving her hand, she said:

"All is bright and happy within the gates of that great city. How they sing praises now!"

The Medium here shaded her eyes for a moment with her hands, then clapped them, and then stood still; and at this moment the Second Medium was again seized by the spirit, (in the language of the believers,) and shouted out, "Come on!"

First Medium—"That's mamma."

Second Medium—"That's you?"

A lady here approached the First Medium, and asked her if she could describe Heaven.

First Medium—"Yes; 'tis with Jesus that I dwell in those regions where angels are ever on the wing."

The Medium here made a motion with her hands, similar to the flapping of wings, accompanying it with the ejaculation, "Ever on the wing, ever on the wing."

Lady—"Do you see grandma?"

"Yes, I see grandma. I think she will be here to-night."

Lady—"Does little Charley want to come back?"

"No, he don't want to come back; the Savior is teaching him."

The Second Medium here commenced striking out her arms in front of her with the most fearful violence. This lasted for some moments, when she changed the motion, and slapped her breast with both hands with great force for about five minutes. Somewhat astonished at this new change of operation, we ejaculated involuntarily something very much like a "halloo, what's to pay now?" and ventured afterwards respectfully to inquire the meaning of these strange movements.

Mr. T.—"The doctor has possession of her now. When he was alive he prescribed for her, and continues to do so now. He has often taken possession of her, and gives her emetics, &c., when necessary. She has now a very bad cold, and he is taking care of her."

Ourself—"Well, this is something new, but we like the idea, and should like to have a doctor on the same terms: for cheapness, if nothing else."

Elderly Lady Medium—"There is too much talking and laughing around the table, and the spirits will be likely to go away."

We were silenced, and just at that moment, the second Medium, whom the doctor was taking care of, suddenly ceased slapping herself, and from the violent contortions of her mouth and face, it was evident that the emetic was in process of being swallowed, and would soon manifest itself in something more than a spiritual manner. It did so; and a moment afterwards, the Medium threw from her mouth a large quantity of phlegm, which it was evident, from her violent coughing sometime previously, ought to have been so thrown off. The doctor was right, and did his duty in the most scientific manner. We consider him a better doctor than many live ones. During all this time, the eyes of our friend in the whiskers were far beyond the line of the longest hair of his facial ornaments.

The Medium now came out of her trance, and Mr. T. had a communication from the spirit of his wife through raps on the table, and spelt out by alphabet. She said she was happy, and was glad to be there and see him.

Both Mediums were now again affected, and the second Medium rose from the table and marched with erect figure and measured tread after the manner of a soldier, drew her imaginary sword and assumed the attitude of command. Thus she spoke:—

"That ain't right. Right to the left, left to the right. Two, four, eight, four to the center, two to the left; eight, face left, forward."

The Medium spoke some time in this way of giving words of command, but the above is enough for example.

We ventured to inquire what spirit had now possession of her, and were answered by the elderly lady, that it was the spirit of Washington, who often came into their circle. The eye of the man with the peaked forehead twinkled with a peculiar twinkle at the intelligence, and our friend of the whiskers was dumb and did not open his mouth; his eyes, however, continued very large. We ourself inquired if Jackson ever came up, and were answered that he did, and Webster also. It was likewise stated that Webster and Clay were in lower spheres than Jackson, to which we slightly demurred, as rather unfair, when we were pleasantly told by the elderly lady Medium that we must not talk politics in the presence of the spirits.

The spirit of Madame Malibran (at least, so we were informed by Mr. T.,) now took possession of the first

Medium, and she commenced talking in a sprightly style and in broken English. Mr. T. informed us that the spirit of Malibran often took possession of both of the Mediums, and that they would play on the piano and sing, and sometimes talk French, although neither of them, when in a natural state, could play, or sing, or speak any language but their own.

The second Medium here suddenly broke out in a rich Irish brogue.

"Faith and how are you Madame Malibran, what makes you look so prim like, devil a bit l care for you."

First Medium.—"How d'do, Patrick, can you talk French?"

Second Medium.—"Devil a bit can I do that same, will you tache me?"

First Medium.—"Yes, I will, good night, I must go, I stay too long."

We here asked who Patrick was, and were informed that it was a funny Irishman named Mulligan, who often took possession of the Medium. We also asked the spirit of Malibran where and when she sang in London, and received for answer, through the Medium, that she did not know, she was so happy in the spirit world that she had forgotten all about what took place when she was in this, and knew only what was going on in this when she came here, as she did that evening. We asked her if she knew any friend of ours in the spirit world, and she answered that she did not, but would inquire for them and tell us another time.

The above was about all of importance that took place at the private circle of Mr. T. In answer to some remarks which we made, Mr. T. informed us that raps were frequent around the house at all hours of the day and night; that he and other members of the family had had astonishing revelations from the spirit world; that they had once been told by the spirits that certain other spirits would, on a certain night, come into the house and fly visibly about in the shape of doves. The day appointed came, and with it came three doves, flying about the room palpably visible, but seeming like illuminated shadows of doves. The candles were withdrawn from the room, but still the doves, with a beautiful halo of light surrounding them, flew noiselessly about the apartment. Mr. T. seems an honest, sincere man; his family and the rest of the persons in the room produced the same impression on us.

CHAPTER IV.

GRAND CIRCLE OF MEDIUMS.

On a certain morning, notwithstanding the heavens above were dark and lowering, and the earth below muddy, splashy and abominably unpleasant to walk upon, we entered the rooms of Mrs. C., the public Rapping Medium, of whom we have before spoken, with our ideas extremely elevated, and our mind in a most sublime and happy state. We felt, in fact, very spiritual, for how could we have felt otherwise; we had been invited to attend a grand spiritual circle, where the circle was to be composed of none but spiritual Mediums, and those Mediums were to be of the fairest part of creation, and no one else. Why, it was enough to make a confirmed Alderman turn spritual, although such a change would have to be set down as the most wonderful miracle since the days of Friar Tuck. Laying aside, however, everything relating to aldermen as not being a very spiritual subject to discourse upon, and confining matters to ourself, we entered, as we said before, Mrs. C.'s rooms very spiritually inclined, because, in view of what we expected to see and hear, we could not help it.

We found the room already half filled, and for some

moments after we entered, those invited came pouring in, until every available spot of space in the room was occupied. There were but few gentlemen present, and after the uncloaking and unbonnetting, and the kisses of greeting between the fair spiritualists had been gone through with, Mrs. C. commenced arranging the circle. Some fifteen of the principal Mediums present, all young women, were placed around the table, while the balance of the company, among whom also there were Mediums, formed at least two more circles, surrounding the first. It was a beautiful and an imposing array. There were Mediums from Boston and Hartford, and many other places, beside New York, and never has it been our privilege and good fortune to look upon a more brilliant collection than they presented, of large, dark, dreamy and flashing, light and laughing eyes; of glossy ringlets and Madona curls, black, brown, auburn and golden, clustering on the sides of cheeks rivalling the bloom of the rose, or parted simply over brows, pale, high, and polished as alabaster. And such a collection of white, tiny and tapering hands as were spread out in a circle on that table! We never before saw so brilliant a display of hands, and we thought within ourself, as our eyes had a battle with themselves, whether they should look the most at the beauty of the faces above or the beauty of the hands below, that if the spirits would not come at the call of such a pressure of such hands as was then inviting them, nothing mortal could bring them.

The circles having been formed, there was silence for

a moment, during which a fair Medium, with a rich profusion of auburn ringlets, which, together with a most exquisite little bonnet, formed a very pretty frame to a very bright face, took a seat at the piano and commenced a plaintive and soothing spiritual song. The whole circle joined in the singing, and the effect was very fine, for all the voices were melodious and the harmony complete. We, ourself, really felt a sort of delicious influence creeping over us as we listened. The reader, however, will remember that we said we felt spiritual before we entered the house, which will account for this susceptibility of ours at the very start.

At the conclusion of the song, the usual question went round the circle of Mediums at the table—"Is any spirit here who will communicate with me?" Strange to say, there was a dead silence—not a rap or sound was heard. Black eyes, blue eyes, hazel eyes—all looked astonished—and there was a great shaking among the curls and ringlets—such a galaxy of Mediums, and not one spirit to answer to their call! it was wonderful. If some stern skeptic had knotted tighter the wrinkles of his face, and asked for a spirit to talk with him, it would have been all very natural for the spirits, in a body, either to repudiate or to snub him; but for the spirits to make no answer to such a grand circle of fair Mediums, it was really too bad; at least we thought so. The question was again passed round, but again there was no answer.

At this moment, a Medium, with a slim, graceful figure, and hair black as jet, parted in Madonna-like curls over a fair forehead, which crowned a face regular in its features and pensive in its expression, was seized with a slight tremor in the hand, and an instant afterwards she seized the pencil and wrote several words with the rapidity of lightning. Then looking at what she wrote, she said in a soft voice, "The spirits say that we must join hands." And the hands were joined, but the result was the same. There was now considerable confusion; some said that the circle was not seated right, and changes were accordingly made; and then several of the Mediums tried, without success, to write, and there were talking and some laughing, varied with small spells of silence, but all to no purpose; the spirits would not come.

At this juncture, a Medium, with full commanding figure, auburn hair plainly dressed, and with large blue and speaking eyes, said: "Sing a song of harmony, that the spirits may be harmonized." Mrs. C. immediately took a seat at the piano, and in a very sweet voice commenced the song "What fairy-like music," &c., and the whole circle, as before, joined in the chorus.

The singing had continued but a short time when our eyes were called from the general survey of the whole circle in which they had been engaged, by the appearance of the Medium with the full figure and auburn hair. She had risen from the table, and now stood rigidly upright, with her eyes fixed as if in a trance of bliss, and her lips moving nervously but uttering no sound. Suddenly her voice burst forth in a high, clear, and rich strain of melody, which silenced all the other voices around her, and caused the looks of all to be turned upon her. The following will serve as a sample of what she sang:

Yes, high is the passage
  To Heaven's bright land,
And Spirits are calling,
  Joining heart and hand.

The love of bright angels
  Descends from on high,
The bright day is shining,
  And Heaven is nigh.

Rejoice! Rejoice! Rejoice!
  Shout to the Heavens above,
In gratitude and love to God,
  For God is love.

As suddenly as she had commenced to sing, she ceased; the fixedness of her eyes relaxed, and she resumed her seat with a shrug, as if she had just awakened from a deep sleep. In answer to our inquiries, we were informed that she remembered nothing of what she had been singing, that it was altogether impromptu, that in fact the spirit was singing through her, and that she was a singing Medium. All we have to say, is that she was a very good singer and something of a poet, whether the spirits inspired her or not.

The spirits (so said to be) seemed to wake up, for there was now a quantity of raps, on the table, under the table, in the corner of the room—in fact all over. But it was impossible to tell who they were for. A spirit here wrote, through one of the Mediums, as follows:

"Many spirits are here from many circles, and they do not harmonize."

At this moment there came three distinct raps on the table, and each one at the table asked if it was for her, and was answered "no." The outside circle then asked the question, and when it came to our turn we were astonished to find that it was for ourself. We then wrote several names of living persons on a paper, and the name of a deceased relative, and pointing to each asked the spirit to designate it. When our pencil pointed to the names of the dead, three raps on the table answered that that one was the spirit now present. We asked the spirit to communicate to us, when the black haired Medium with the Madonna curls caught hold of the pencil to write, but after considerable trembling of the hand, gave it up, and we received no communication.

One of the Mediums here asked the Spirits if they would have the kindness to tell why those present had not more satisfactory manifestations. No sooner was the question asked, than one of the Mediums, Miss E., dressed in black, with black hair, high forehead, pale features, and large spiritual-looking eyes, was seized with a trembling of her whole frame, which soon gave place to a calm rigidity, and with her eyes fixed, as if on a vacancy before her, she spoke (by the direction, as it is said, of a spirit,) as follows:—

"Those assembled here are harmonious, but each has a different motive, and one Medium depends too much on the other—not passive enough. I could speak vol umes, but there are many excellent spirits to speak with you all. I desire that each one of you should ask questions, for every individual here has attracted a congenial spirit."

Having spoken thus, the Medium recovered herself in pretty much the same manner as the singing Medium had done before her.

Whether in answer to the spirit who spoke through Miss E., or not, we are unable to tell, but certain it is that when Miss E. ceased speaking, Mrs. C. also went off in a trance, her eyes became closed, and she groped around the room, touching every one with her hands, until she came to a fine looking woman dressed in black, who (we have forgotten to mention it before) had previously been asking, at several times, in an affectionate voice, if her little daughter would communicate with her. When Mrs. C. reached this lady she laid her hands gently on her forehead, as if in the act of blessing, and then left her, went to the table, opened her eyes, raised them upwards, then seized a pencil, traced some words on a piece of paper, then went to another table and returned with a small miniature, which she laid on the table the circle surrounded. At this moment the cheeks of the lady in black became deadly pale, her whole frame appeared convulsed, and she broke forth into deep and heavy sobs. So violently was she affected, that she was borne from the room, but was soon brought back somewhat calmed, but still apparently unconscious of what was going on around her. Suddenly the singing Medium with the auburn hair, rose, faced the mother, and extending her hand over her in a majestic attitude, sang in the same clear rich voice as before:

> Weep not, mother dear,
> When Spirits of infants are near,
> For words they bring of good cheer.
>
> Thus can I approach thee, mother dear,
> Glad song of love I bring thee,
> When I am hovering near.
>
> Love! Love! is a beautiful thing,
> Heaven is open to man,
> Rejoice, mother dear, while I sing,
> And my spirit is hovering near.

Much more she sang in the same strain, and the tune, which was a beautiful one, is not, we venture to say, set down in any of the books. The mother awakened with a smile, from her trance, and the Medium resumed her seat.

Mrs. C. again went off in a walking trance with closed eyes; but this time she laid her hands on a short stout gentleman in spectacles and whiskers and a very small slightly elevated nose, bearing no affinity to the classical pattern of either Greece or Rome. It was truly an American independent nose, built after a pattern and on a broad full moon foundation of face peculiarly its own. We may as well here remark, according to the information which we received on the subject, that in the blind walking trance which now had full possession of Mrs. C., the disciples of spiritualism believed that a spirit wished to communicate with some one in the room—that the spirit through Mrs. C. would point out the desired person, and lead him to the Medium through whom the spirit wished to speak to him. Mrs. C. picked out the gentleman with the spectacles and the little nose, and having picked him out, she passed her hand gently over his forehead, which operation, the gentleman with the spectacles and the nose seemed to like greatly; for his eyes twinkled brightly through his glasses, and the elevation of the tip of his little nose seemed (we may have imagined it) to be greatly increased. Leaving his forehead, the hands of Mrs. C. sought those of him of the spectacles and the nose, which having found, she led and seated him, by the side of one of the most spiritual-looking Mediums in the room, and placed the hands of the latter in his. It was a beautiful little hand and soft as velvet, and while the brilliancy of eyelight, gleamed more intensely than ever through the spectacles, the little nose this time fairly trembled. There was a blush also on his face; for he seemed a bashful young man, and altogether he was in a very nervous position. With the most profound respect, however, he bent over the hand which he held, and waited for the voice of the spirit through the Medium. The hand of the latter trembled violently for a few moments, and she seemed as if she also was going into a trance; but it passed off, and he of the nose and spectacles retired to his position outside of the table, no wiser than before.

More songs were sung—more attempts made to gain

some remarkable manifestations; but without avail. The general opinion seemed to be that too many Mediums were present, and that the eagerness of all to have communications, was productive of a want of harmony, which prevented any great test manifestation from taking place.

CHAPTER V.

THE EVIL SPIRITS.

In our tour among the Spiritual Rapping Circles of New York, we a few evenings since paid a second visit to the private circle at the house of Mr. T. We found the room and table, as before, crowded. The two young girl Mediums were there and were seated at the table, waiting, we presume, for spirits to take possession of them. The rest of the company consisted mainly of the same persons whom we had before seen there. Two individuals particularly attracted our attention; the one was a pale-faced gentleman with a goat (we beg pardon—we mean a small tuft of cultivated hair,) under his chin; and the other was a gentleman rotund in person, with a broad face, rosy in complexion, and beaming with good nature. He with the pale face and the goat looked as if his mind was ever on the stretch of inquiry, while he of the rosy face looked as if he generally kept his mind perfectly easy, and was not in the habit of stretching it on any but extraordinary occasions. Having taken our seat, we remained silent with the rest of the circle, during a space of some five minutes, in which the spirits were waited for, but did not come.

The silence was broken by the gentleman with the

goat, who addressed to the gentleman with the rosy face some remarks on the subject of spiritual rappings, which led to a short animated conversation between the two parties. The gentleman with the goat was a firm believer not only in spiritual rappings, but in mesmerism, clairvoyance, psychology, and all unto each of these appertaining. He evidently went in for all the new doctrines of the day, and was profoundly impressed with the belief that he knew something of each. The gentleman with the rosy face, however, was to us a puzzle. We could not tell whether he believed in Spiritual Rappings or not, and although he talked freely and pleasantly, when he was through, the company were about as wise in regard to his real opinions as they were before he opened his mouth. He was evidently of the non-committal order of men, and was therefore a wise man.

The learned conversation of the above parties was at length interrupted by the appearance of both the girl Mediums, who, by the nervous motions of their hands and the twitchings of the muscles of their faces, gave evidence that they were about to be taken possession of (as it is said) by spirits. The hands of both were soon thrashing up and down the edge of the table in the same manner as we have previously described it in the account of our first visit to the house of Mr. T. This violent motion soon subsided, and then the Mediums suddenly locked their right hands together and extended them towards the man with the rosy face.

"Well, and what do you want with me?" said he of

the rosy face. "Is there any spirit wishes to communi cate with me?"

The Mediums opened not their mouths, but knocked their hands on the table, as much as to say "Yes."

Although the Mediums would not speak, it was suggested to the man with the rosy face that he should ask whatever questions he saw fit, and wait for his answer, in whatever form he might get it. He did so by writing down the Christian names of several living persons and one dead one, and then pointing to each successively, he asked the Mediums if that was the spirit which wished to communicate with him. When he pointed to the Christian name of the dead person, the hands of the Mediums thumped three times on the table, meaning thereby "Yes." The man with the rosy face looked rather astonished; for he alone in the room saw the names which he had written, or knew which belonged to the living or dead. The answer, however, was right, and the man with the rosy face, still further to test the matter, now wrote on another slip of paper the surnames belonging to the Christian ones. The hands of the Mediums thumped "Yes" at the right surname. The man with the rosy face looked still more astonished, and proceeded to put more questions, but did not receive much more information, except that the spirit was his guardian spirit, and would communicate with him further at some future period.

The mediums now suddenly unlocked their hands, the eldest girl recovered her consciousness; but the younger one rose from the table with all the features of her face convulsively twitching, and her arms thrashing wildly around her. She appeared at the same time to be in pain and distress, and in the act of a desperate resistance to some evil influence. We ourself felt alarmed, and many, even of the firm believers at the table who are seldom frightened at what they see, appeared to us as if they did not feel quite at their ease. The man with the goat looked calmly on with an inquiring, but not a troubled eye, while he with the rosy face rather quickly said :

"For God sake, what does all this mean? She will hurt herself; stop it if possible."

Some one here suggested that it was probably some evil spirit which had taken possession of the Medium, and an effort was made, but in vain, to hold her.

"It is probably an undeveloped spirit," here remarked the man with the goat, "and probably I may so impress her, after the psychological manner, as to cause it to leave her," and the man with the goat made some few other remarks in the same strain.

"Suppose you try your hand, and see if your theory is right," said he with the rosy face to him with the goat.

The man with the goat rose very deliberately from his chair, approached the girl Medium, looked steadfastly in her face, and said pretty much as follows :—"Evil spirit, please leave this young woman; retire, go away, you are subjecting her to distress; will you therefore depart?"

not very profitable to talk to evil people on earth in such a polite manner as this; but that commanding, knock-down methods of speech were more effective, and he supposed that evil spirits also required something stronger than polite requests.

The girl Medium, in the meantime, thrashed about as wildly as ever, and the man with the goat took his seat, with the knowledge that the evil or undeveloped spirit, whichever it may have been, was too much for him.

"I have a mind," said the man with the rosy face, rising from his seat, "to try my hand now. I don't know that I shall accomplish anything, but I am curious to make the trial."

Thus speaking, he approached the girl, stood before her in a commanding attitude, looked her steadily in the face, and making before her, with his hand, the sign of the cross, said in a stern voice:

"If you are an evil spirit that possesses this young girl, I command you, in the name of the Father, Son, and Holy Ghost, to leave her."

In an instant, the arms of the girl dropped loosely by her side, the rigid tension of the whole muscles of her frame ceased, her face assumed its usual calm expression, she sank into a chair, closed her eyes for a moment, and then opened them again with a confused look around the room, as if she had just awakened from a sleep. She remembered nothing of what she had been doing, or of what had been going on around her.

The above striking incident formed the occasion of considerable conversation among the company. A very pleasant old lady, in a neat cap, and whom we alluded to in a former account of this circle, as being a Medium, remarked that the girl Medium had been violently seized by an evil spirit before, and that she had been quieted by the reading of the bible; to which remark he of the rosy face answered that he did not doubt that the reading of the bible would do just as well as what he had done, that he had only used, by way of experiment, the old form employed by the Primitive Church to exorcise evil spirits, and that the company had seen the result.

He of the rosy face soon afterwards retired, and we accompanied him, and have written down the account of this incident in our Spiritual Rapping tour, just as it oçcurred.

THE CIRCLE IN DARK.

In company with a well-known public Medium, and with a friend whose faith in Spiritual Rappings has no limits to its fervor and sincerity, we paid a visit to the house of a private Medium, where, we were told, the table was in the habit of performing curious antics, and where strange spiritual lights were to be seen. After the ceremony of our introduction was over, and we were made acquainted with the Medium and several others who joined the circle, the room was darkened, and the spirits asked if they would make themselves manifest. The table immediately began to tip and dance about, raps were heard on it, and finally it was raised above the heads of the party, lowered down, legs uppermost, and then returned to its right position. The table was a small mahogany one, and no hands of the party present had any agency in moving it. Of this we feel assured. In the meantime, one of the Mediums present —for there were several—exclaimed, "See what beautiful lights on the table!" We looked, and saw something in the shape of a small star flickering around the table, but whether it came from a crack in the door or window, or was a reflection of some glass, we could not decide; it looked very pretty, however, and might well pass for a spiritual manifestation. In the meantime, several present exclaimed that they were touched by the spirits, and among the rest our friend with the boundless faith. We were asked if we had not felt our self touched, but not having to our knowledge been thus honored, we were obliged to respond "No."

No other manifestations of any consequence took place in the circle in the dark, and we returned home. On our way, in talking to our friend with the boundless faith, we remarked that we had heard that he had many wonderful communications from the spirits, some of them quite amusing.

"Spirits are sometimes jocular as well as mortals," he answered, with the most perfect simplicity, "as witness what I had one day just before dinner. The communication was written as follows:

"'Friend, it is about dinner time; don't forget your dinner; go right off to your dinner.

(Signed) BOOTH.'"

"And," added our friend, "the signature was hardly traced before a postscript was added:

"'Yes; don't forget your dinner, and go to Windust's. (Signed) HAMBLIN.'"

CHAPTER VI.

THE SPIRIT OF THE REV. JOHN N. MAFFIT.

During our investigations into the subject of Spiritual Rappings, we often had occasion to visit the rooms of Mr. C., the public Tipping Medium, whom we have before spoken of in the first chapter of this book. We think it was at our second or third visit, that we were particularly struck with a gentleman present who was completely in a fog with reference to a spirit that expressed its desire to communicate with him. We saw the same gentleman almost every time we visited Mr. C., and he was in the same fog about the same spirit until on a certain night, the fog, in some measure, cleared away. As there is considerable singularity ahout the manœuvres of this gentlemnn in the fog, with the spirit which befogged him, we shall relate all about tne matter, as far as we ourself was an actual witness.

The gentleman to whom we have alluded above, and whom, for want of a more distinctive appellation, we shall call the gentleman in the fog, appeared before us, when we first saw him, as a very pleasant personage to look upon. He was dressed in deep black, his forehead was high, and gave evidence of intellect; his eyes were large, very expressive, and the light which shone out from them was not at all obscured by a light pair of steel spectacles. His face was round and full, encircled with well laid out and thickly populated black whiskers; his person was stout and well conditioned, and in addition to the intellect exhibited by his head, his whole air denoted that he was one of the best natured fellows in the world. His hands rested reverentially on the table, and his look around was curious and inquiring. We at once set him down as an investigator, which opinion was confirmed, when in answer to a question put to him as to whether or not he believed in Spiritual Rappings, he answered :

"I neither believe nor disbelieve, have not any opinion about it, am open to conviction, open to all kinds of knowledge from spirits in the spirit land and mortals in this; the spirits may talk to me, or knock on me, or grasp me, or rap around me, do anything they please, only if they will identify themselves as spirits it will be all I ask of them, so let them come on and give proof, that's what I am after; therefore, Mr. C., if you have no objection, I will now ask if there is any spirit here who wishes to communicate with me ?" And the gentleman in the fog had no sooner uttered these last words, than the table tipped up and thumped very emphatically three times, meaning thereby to say "yes."

"Well," said the gentleman in the fog, "if I write some names on several slips of paper, will you tell me whether either of them is the spirit now present ?"

The answer to this question was "yes," and the gentleman wrote several names of living persons and the name of one dead one on slips of paper, rolled them tightly up, threw them on the table, and then pointing to each successfully, asked if that was the one. The table tipped three times to one of the slips of paper, and the gentleman in the fog took it up, and was about opening it, when Mr. C. suggested that before he opened it he had better ask the spirit to spell out by alphabet the name on the paper. The question was asked, the spirit (so-called) answered "yes," and the calling of the alphabet having been commenced, a name was spelt out, which, on being compared to that in the paper, proved to be the same, and the name of the only dead person among those written on the several slips of paper. The gentleman in the fog here asked many questions of the spirit who professed to be communicating with him, but from the expression of his face and the twinkle of his eyes under his spectacles, we were under the impression that he thought that the answers did not amount to much.

At this moment Mr. C.'s arm began to quiver, and his fingers to twitch, as if he was in haste to beat a lightning tatoo. Having, however, grasped a pencil, the lightning tatoo resolved itself into a lightning dispatch by writing, which, being finshed by an eccentric whirl of the pencil, read as follows:

DEAR FRIEND—I am glad you are investigating this subject. Go on, I will aid you.

(Signed,) JOHN.

"For whom is that?" said the gentleman in the fog.

"For you," answered Mr. C.; and the table gave three loud tips, as if in endorsement of Mr. C.'s words.

"For me?" said the gentleman in the fog, and his eyes opened so wide that a semi-circle of white ap peared above and below the rims of his spectacles. "For me?—pshaw! you must be mistaken; I do not know any dead John."

Again the table gave three bumping tips, as much as to say that the gentleman in the fog was mistaken, and that he did know a dead John.

"I do *not* know you, friend John," again reiterated the gentleman in the fog, and again came three bumps of the table, meaning that the gentleman in the fog *did* know friend John.

The gentleman in the fog here, very resolutely, took his hands from the table, and, running them deep into his pantaloons' pockets, leaned back and said, "This is very strange: I emphatically assert that I do *not* know this John, and he insists that I do. Well, I will ask him one more question. Friend John, will you have the kindness to tell me your surname?"

The table answered with two tips, meaning thereby, "Not now."

The fog gathered deeper and deeper about the gentleman in the fog, and he appeared to be nonplussed. But he tried again—

"Friend John, will you tell me your surname?"

"Yes."

"Will you tell me here?"

"No."

"Will you tell me up at my house?"

"No."

"Will you come up to my house and rap on the head-board of my bed?"

"Yes."

"Am I a Medium?"

"Yes," and the three tips this time almost turned the table over.

"When will you come up and rap at my house—within a week?"

"Yes."

"Will you spell out your name by alphabet when you tell it to me?"

"No."

"How, then, shall I find it out? Will it flash across my mind, and you then confirm it?"

"Yes."

"Have you anything more to say now?"

"No."

"Then good-bye, friend John, and permit me to say you are a very curious fellow."

And, as the gentleman in the fog bid John adieu, the semi-circle of white above and below his spectacles was very large, and the fog was so thick before him that he evidently thought he could cut it with a knife.

Such is a literal account of what we heard and saw when we first met the gentleman in the fog at Mr. C.'s table.

Two weeks elapsed, and again we met the gentleman in the fog at Mr. C.'s. He was still in the fog, and sat back from the table, looking very inquiringly on, but asking no questions.

Snddenly, however, the table tipped very loudly three times, and, all around it having asked if it was a spirit for any of them, and having been answered it was not, the gentleman in the fog very modestly remarked that possibly it might be some spirit for him—perhaps friend John.

The table now fairly danced, as much as to say that the spirit was for the gentleman in the fog, and was no other than the veritable John.

Like a warrior buckling up his armor before he goes forth to the fight, the gentleman in the fog buttoned up his coat, drew his chair up to the table, and prepared to attack John this time in right earnest.

"Friend John," he said, "you stick to me like wax; now manifest yourself—tell who you are."

C.'s arm and hands were immediately no bad imitation of chain-lightning, and the express, when deciphered, read as follows:

My Dear Friend—I am the individual against whom, while on earth, you wrote so severely. You did me an injury while on earth, and I am now here to do good for evil. (Signed,) John.

"John, you are mistaken; I have never written against any John in any newspaper."

The table tipped that John was not mistaken, and the tips were emphatic.

"John, how have I written severely about you—give me some clue?"

The answer, written through the hand of Mr. C., was as follows:

"You were not aware of what you were doing; you wrote unthinkingly."

"I did not do it then maliciously?"

And again the answer came in writing:

"No; you did it to make a good article: you newspaper people are the kindest people in the world."

"John, you are rather satirical."

"Yes, sir."

"But, John, how are you going to return to me good for evil?"

"By helping you to investigate this subject, and making you of service to mankind."

John said much more to the gentleman in the fog, and another spirit (so-called) made a communication in writing to the gentleman in the fog, signing the initials B. D., and telling him that he (the gentleman in the fog) was destined to be a shining light in Spiritualism, and that he (the spirit B. D.) would help John in serving the gentleman in the fog in his investigations after spiritual truth.

"But, John," again said the gentleman in the fog, "you have not yet told me your name; you are all wrong—I never knew you, never wrote a line against any John, and it strikes me, John, (excuse me if I use a very common word here on the earth) it strikes me that you are humbugging me."

The table tipped "No."

"But I think you are, John; you have told me what was not true; others may have abused you in newspapers, but I never have, and besides you promised to come and rap on my bed and you have not, and above all you resolutely refused to tell me your surname so that I can identify you. Now, once for all, John, will you tell me your surname at this moment and satisfy me?"

"No!" was the answer tapped by the table, and then the circle broke up, and the gentleman in the fog departed with the rest.

A few evenings after this, we were sitting with Mr. C. and a full circle, around the table of Mrs. B., the public Rapping Medium of whom we have before spoken. On looking about, we found that the gentleman in the fog was seated next to us, and in answer to a question whether he was still in a fog with reference to his friend John, he answered with a pleasant smile, "Yes." Beside the gentleman in the fog, there was another person in the circle who attracted our attention. This was a lady, delicate in figure, with very black hair and eyes, and a full supply of flowers on the inside border of her pretty little bonnet. The lady was evidently an unbeliever, for she twirled her pencil in her white little hand, and said with an air of slight contempt—

"I have never had any satisfactory communications, and the spirits, as they call them, have told me some most tremendous untruths;" and then turning to an intelligent looking gentleman at the table, she asked, "Do you think, sir, that spirits would lie?"

"It is not impossible," or something to that effect, was the answer; "finite beings are not always truthful, and spirits not yet developed, may possibly speak falsely. I do not think it strange, perhaps there is no one at this table, who has not either uttered or thought an untruth to-day. No one is perfect and all spirits are not."

The lady in the black hair and the flowery bonnet drew up slightly a very pretty mouth, and said that she did not think she had uttered or thought, that day, an untruth, and that she did not agree with the gentleman's doctrine about the spirits.

The gentleman, here referred to, now asked some questions mentally, which were answered by frequent and loud rappings, which appeared to us to be under the table, but which he said were on his foot. What the questions were we did not learn, but the answers to them appeared to be satisfactory to the asker. He had also a communication from his brother, spelt out by the alphabet, which was very pretty both in language and sentiment. Each one around the table now successively questioned the spirits, until it came to the turn of the gentleman in the fog.

"Is there any spirit here for me?" asked the gentleman in the fog, and "yes" was the answer rapped on the table directly in front of the gentleman in the fog.

"Is John here?"

And three loud raps conveyed the information that John was again on hand.

"John, will you tell me your surname now?"

"Yes."

"Will you spell it out?"

"No."

"If I write down a number of surnames, will you rap at the right one?"

"Yes."

The gentleman in the fog, as if some sudden idea had struck him, wrote down several surnames, so that no one but himself could see them, and then pointing with his pencil to each, asked the spirit to rap at the right one.

The rap came, and the gentleman looked rather surprised, and said:

"John, can you identify yourself to me?"

The answer spelt out by alphabet was:

"I can convince you by fair testing."

"Well, do it."

And again the answer, spelt out by alphabet, was as follows, directed to Mrs. B.:

"I will give him some hard knocks if you let some one hold your feet."

Mrs. B. here expressed a wish that the gentleman in the fog would not hold any further communication with this spirit, as she feared it was not a very good one, but the gentleman in the fog thought John would turn out a pretty good spirit after all.

"John," he said, "I wave the holding of Mrs. B.'s

feet, so knock me as hard as you please and make yourself manifest."

But there were no knocks from John on the person of the gentleman in the fog, but the alphabet was called for by the spirit, and the following communication spelt out:

"My Friend—I am a preacher. I wish I had ten thousand tongues, and I would undo all the wrongs I did when I lived in your sphere. I could easily identify myself if you remember the scar. I cling to you, as you appear to be a sincere seeker after truth. I am happy to manifest my presence to circles who are unprejudiced and charitable to all. God is merciful to all his children, and before his throne I humbly bow in prayer for all who are willing to be blessed."

"(Signed,) "J. M."

"Does the initial of the surname correspond to that which you wrote and to which the spirit rapped?" asked Mrs. B.

"Yes," answered the gentleman in the fog, "and the name I suppose is John Maffit, who was once a celebrated Methodist preacher, for I wrote the surname of Maffit on the slip of paper, and the spirit picked it out. The name flashed across my mind and I wrote it."

The table gave three loud raps in confirmation of the words of the gentleman in the fog.

"But," said he, "I never saw Mr. Maffit when alive. Has he a scar?"

Some gentleman at the table answered that Maffit had one on his lip.

"Did you have a middle name?" said the gentleman in the fog; addressing himself to the so-called spirit.

"Yes."

And the correct name was indicated by raps, several other names having been written down with it and pointed to with a small pencil, as before.

"Now, John, answer me these questions—did I ever see you?"

"No."

"Did I ever persecute you?"

"No."

"Have you anything more to say?"

"No."

"Then good night," and the gentleman in the fog bid the circle good evening and departed.

Whether the gentleman in the fog is in the fog still, we are at present unadvised, but we have written down the whole spiritual scenes in regard to John and the gentleman in the fog, just as they occurred, and thus place them before the reader.

CHAPTER VII.

OLIVER BLODGE, THE MURDERER.

ONE afternoon, having partaken, with great zeal and zest, of an excellent dinner, and feeling perfectly at peace "with all the world and the rest of mankind," we were consequently in a most fit frame of mind to listen complacently and impartially to any information which might turn up concerning the world of spirits as interpreted by the Spirit Rappers, into the mysteries of whose faith we were making our philosophical investi gations. It was our fortune, while the good effects of our good dinner were still pleasantly with us, to drop into the office of a friend, where the mysteries of Spiritual Rappings and Table Tippings and Turnings were in process of being discussed, and we accordingly pricked up our ears and prepared, in the language of the immortal Mr. Bunsby, to "make a note of it." The party at our friend's office exhibited among its members just such a variety of opinions on the subject under discussion, as to render the conversation very entertaining, and withal extremely unctuous. On the faces of several of the persons present there was a pleasant smile of incredulity; one or two looked slightly contemptuous;

some presented on their countenances a sort of either-way-edness expression, strikingly suggestive of the idea of a fence with a sitting occupant of an accommodating disposition; some looked trusting and believing, others wonder-struck, while one individual leaned back cozily in his chair, and with his hands folded comfortably over a most portly corporeal rotundity, presented to the gaze of the company a round expanse of face, which we cannot better describe than by saying that it seemed a perfect blank as far as it exhibited any index of the workings of his mind.

The principal speaker in the party was a man of intellectual appearance, and although the flaxen moustache and imperial, which graced his upper lip and chin, gave evidence that he heartily repudiated all modern hair-dyes, the zeal and earnestness with which he spoke, showed that his soul was thoroughly colored with the dye of Modern Spiritualism, that he loved the dye, and had no desire to wash it out.

While the man with the flaxen moustache and imperial was in the midst of an animated account of his experience in spiritual manifestation, the portly man with the blank face suddenly roused himself up and exclaimed in a jocular tone:

"Now you do not believe all you have been saying, do you? are you not given to dreaming when you are awake?"

"Believe it, sir? as firmly as I stand here. I cannot help believing it, because I have had such astonishing and convincing proofs: and besides, I wish to believe in Spiritualism, for the spirits have done me an immense deal of good."

"Done you good! how?"

"In more ways than one; why, it is but a few days ago that a spirit took away my cigar, and I have not smoked since."

"Took away your cigar? Please give us that story in full," and there was a slight twinkle in the eye of the man with the blank face, as he made this request.

"The story," answered the man with the flaxen moustache and imperial, "is simply this. I was smoking one day while I was writing at my table, and having occasion to get up for a moment, I laid the cigar down on the table, and when an instant after I reached out my hand to pick the cigar up again, it was gone. There was no other person but myself in the room, and no one but a spirit could have taken the cigar away so mysteriously. I considered it as an intimation from a spirit that it was best for me not to smoke, and I have not since, and I feel better for it."

"Well, you will do," answered the man with the blank face. "You have gone in, I see, completely, moustache, imperial, and all; but, by the by, as you must know all about the Spiritual Rappers, can you tell me anything about a certain spirit called Oliver Blodge, the murderer? I have begun to investigate a little this table rapping and turning business, and since I commenced I have heard considerable about one Oliver Blodge, a rather remarkable spirit (as he is called) who has made some queer manifestations in certain circles. What do you know about him?"

"A great deal," answered the man with the flaxen moustache and imperial; "I have seen him, and I will tell you all I know about him. There is in this city a highly respectable private circle of spiritualists with whom I am acquainted, and among whom are some musicians and actors of note. They meet once a week, and have had some wonderful manifestations. Among other spirits who have been in the habit of communicating with this circle, that of Ben Jonson has been one of the most frequent. He has manifested himself under four different names, one of which is O'Shucks. Mr. S., a member of the circle, who is a good medium, has been often favored particularly with the communications of O'Shucks,—in fact O'Shucks declared himself to be the guardian spirit of Mr. S., and Mr. S. received and acknowledged him as such. At some of the earliest meetings of this circle to which I refer, besides the spirit of O'Shucks, another remarkable spirit manifested himself, signing his name Oliver Blodge, and making some communications not very choice in language or pure in tone. When questioned as to who and what he had been while he was in his mortal form, he answered very bluntly that he had been hung for murder, some half a century ago."

We will continue this part of the narrative of the man with the moustache, in our language.

From the time Blodge thus announced his character, he kept continually thrusting himself, as above referred to, on the circle, making communications at inopportune times—making them sometimes in profane and sometimes in abusive language, and always so manifesting himself as to render himself disagreeable to the circle; although frequently, even in his outrageous communications, he was amusing. At length, one evening, when the circle were seated, Blodge took possession of Mr. S., and wrote out through his hand as follows:—

"Wouldn't you like me better than O'Shucks for your guardian spirit?"

Mr. S. answered that he "liked O'Shucks very well."

"But wouldn't you like me as well?" asked Blodge.

Mr. S., in a laughing way, returned "Yes" for answer.

"Then won't you take me for your guardian spirit, for O'Shucks is a humbug?" again asked Blodge.

"Oh, yes," again laughingly answered Mr. S.

"Then write down on a piece of paper that you will do so," said Blodge.

Mr. S. did as Blodge requested, and asked the latter if he saw what he had written.

"Yes," answered Blodge, "but that is not enough—you must sign it."

Mr. S. made the required signature of his name, and "ever since that time," said the man with the flaxen moustache and imperial, laying great emphasis on his words, "O'Shucks has not been able to communicate through Mr. S., so completely has Blodge monopolized him. S. indeed signs O'Shucks' name sometimes to communications written through his hand, but it is

Blodge who does it, and counterfeits O'Shucks' signature."

"Terrible!" exclaimed, at this point of the narrative, the man with the blank face, who had paid the most strict attention to all the above account of Blodge the murderer, given by the man with the moustache and imperial. "However," continued he of the blank face, "I like to hear it. Is there any more to come? I think you said you saw the spirit of this awful Oliver Blodge."

"So I did," answered he of the moustache. "Wait a minute and I will come to that part. Soon after Blodge had thus, as I have said, taken a monopoly of the Medium, Mr. S., and made it a practice to counterfeit O'Shucks' name through the hand of Mr. S., another Medium, who was in the habit of attending the circle, had a spiritual communication which told him the secret of discovering when O'Shucks' name was forged by Blodge. And at a subsequent meeting of the circle, the Medium referred to, by way of experiment, asked Mr. S. if he could give the signature of O'Shucks, as he had before been in the habit of doing before Blodge had obtained control of him.—Mr. S. answered that he could, but the other Medium doubting, asked him to try. Mr. S. took a pencil, and after a convulsive effort wrote the name O'Shucks. The Medium took the paper, examined it, and said, "This is not O'Shucks' signature; try again." Mr. S. did so several times, and each time the forgery of O'Shucks' name was detected. The Medium now commanded the spirit, in the name of the living God, to write his (the spirit's) own name. And immediately, through the hand of Mr. S., was written the name 'Oliver Blodge.' The Medium then again addressed Blodge, in the name of the living God, and defied him to write again the name of O'Shucks. Mr. S. was immediately convulsed, his pencil moved over the paper without writing anything, and Oliver Blodge was overcome in his forging propensities. At this time all at the table felt an unpleasant influence about them, and I myself, who was present, although I did not see anything, felt as if a form, not mortal, was by me, and that form was Oliver Blodge."

"Then you did not *see* Oliver, after all," exclaimed the man with the blank face, as he slightly shifted the position of his folded hands and looked up inquiringly.

"Do not be in quite such a hurry; I *did see* Oliver Blodge, but not then. A few days after this occurrence at the circle, when I was alone in my room, and wide awake as I am now, I saw a form standing in the corner of the room, which I knew at once to be the spirit of Oliver Blodge. His face was disgusting and revolting to look at—red, livid and bloated, and he had a green patch over one of his eyes. He was dressed in a coarse pea-jacket, such as I suppose he wore when he was in mortal form on the earth. I did not wish to have any thing to do with such a spirit—so I commanded him, with a strong effort of my will, to go, and not come to me again. He disappeared with a whirl, and on looking a moment afterwards at the bell-wire, near which he had stood, I found that it was all twisted into a heap, and no other but the spirit of Oliver Blodge could have done it."

"He was probably very mad because you sent him away so unceremoniously," said the man with the blank face, and the conversation on spiritualism in our friend's office then came to a close.

The above was what we heard from the gentleman with the flaxen moustache and imperial, in reference to the spirit of Oliver Blodge, the murderer. We come now to what we ourself were witness to in regard to the same so-called spirit.

A few evenings after the above conversation, in our friend's office, we visited the residence of Mr. J. F. W., and were introduced to a private circle of spiritualists, who were in the habit of assembling there. On looking around, we discovered that a very worthy public Medium of this city was present, and also our acquaintance, the man with the blank face, whom we had seen at our friend's office when the man with the flaxen moustache and imperial gave his experience in regard to the spirit of Oliver Blodge.

Although all the persons (consisting about equally of ladies and gentlemen) assembled at Mr. W.'s circle were plainly of intellectual and refined character, we were particularly struck with two individuals. The one was a young lady in the bloom of youth and beauty. With dark glossy hair parted in graceful curls over her clear and noble forehead, beneath which two piercing black eyes looked laughingly and kindly out from under long silken eye-lashes, and with a whole expression of countenance which said plainly that she was possessed of a lively intellect and great amiability of disposition, we thought that the spirit could not choose a more perfect Medium to communicate with mortals, if indeed they do hold such communication. We were informed that she was a Medium, through whom the spirits not only spoke, but to whom they manifested themselves in visible shape and form. The other person who attracted our attention, was a middle-aged man, whose peculiar characteristics were a subdued manner when talking of or to the spirits, and an eye which beamed with kindness and sensibility. He was a firm believer in spiritualism.

"Is there any spirit here who wishes to communicate with me?" asked abruptly the man with the blank face.

The table, which was a large circular mahogany one, tipped emphatically "yes."

"Who is it?" and the words had hardly left his mouth, before the hand of the Public Medium, whom we have noticed as being present, was immediately seized by the supposed spirit, and the hand wrote the name "Oliver Blodge."

"Ah, Oliver, you are here, are you?" said he of the blank face, very composedly.

"Yes, and mean to stick to you," was the answer written out by the hand of the Public Medium whom we have before mentioned. (We may as well say here that all the answers by Oliver Blodge to the man with the blank face were written through the hands of this Medium.)

"You mean to stick to me?" said he of the blank face. "Well, do so; and now give me some physical manifestation of your presence."

"You'll have it on your head soon."

"Well, do it now."

But the promised manifestation on the head of the man with the blank face, was not given.

"Oliver," continued the man with the blank face, "I am afraid you are a bad fellow. Were you a murderer, and is all that I heard a gentleman tell about you the other day, in my friend's office, true?"

"Yes."

"Oliver, do you fear God?"

"I have yet to find Him."

"Then you have never seen God?"

"No."

"Do you expect to see Him?"

"Don't know."

"Then you do not fear Him?"

"Now listen to my answer. I do not fear God for the same reason that I love Him."

"A very good answer, Oliver, for you to make; but, Oliver, give me some test that you are the spirit you represent yourself to be."

"Look under your chair."

The man with the blank face looked under his chair, and after looking in vain for something, said:

"Oliver, there is nothing there."

"Neither is there anything in your head," was Oliver's

answer. The man with the blank face evidently had the worst of it at this point of the conversation.

"Oliver," continued he of the blank face, "you are fooling me."

"Yes, birds of a feather flock together."

"Why, you do not mean to say that I am a murderer?'

"Yes, a murderer of common sense."

"Will you tell me how I have murdered common sense?"

"No, because you have not progressed far enough to comprehend it if I should tell you; you want something which you are very much in need of."

"What is that?"

"You want more confidence in spirits and less in theology."

"Do you think I am a churchman?"

"You are worse; your mind is shackled by the gall ing chains of error and superstition, because you suppose that the invocation of the Trinity can cast out evil spirits."

"You are still severe on me, Oliver."

"I wish to pump you full and then drain you off at leisure."

"What will be left when you have done?"

"An apology for common sense."

"Do you mean to say that I have no common sense?"

"I mean to say that you are full of common, and short of sense."

"What do you mean by the common, of which you say I am full?"

"Early prejudice."

"What sort of a fellow am I, any way?"

"One whom the spirits will soon handle as they please."

"Favorably?"

"Yes."

"Oliver, have you gone yet?"

"No; and you'll find out soon that I have only just begun."

"You say that you are going to stick to me. Do you intend to try to exert a bad influence over me?"

"My business is to get the bark off."

"Is there any bark about me?"

"Yes, and considerable wind, too."

"You are getting saucy, Oliver; and as you will not let me see you, I would ask how you look?"

"Like hell and the devil."

"Oliver Blodge, you are a bad spirit, and I wish you would retire; I do not wish to say anything more to you."

"I only mentioned those names to see what effect, a devil, which is not to be found, and a hell which has no existence, would have upon you."

"What sphere are you in, Oliver?"

"I never learned to count, but should judge that I was in sympathy with you; but my friend, you are a fine fellow, and will one day make a fine spirit."

"Oliver, are you happy?"

"Ask the mariner if he rejoices at the dawn of a beautiful morning, after having been tempest-tossed for weeks."

"Will you let me see you, Oliver?"

"I would willingly, if you would disperse the mist of doubt which intervenes."

During the above conversation between the man with the blank face and the so-called spirit of Oliver Blodge, the lady Medium, with the dark hair and bright eyes, frequently remarked, as she gazed apparently on vacancy, that she distinctly saw before her the spirit of Blodge. When he first appeared in the circle, she said that he stood behind the chair of the Medium through whom he was writing, and that he was dressed in a pea-jacket, had a patch over his eye, but that his face was not very repulsive. During the communications between him and the man with the blank face, she said that Blodge frequently changed his position, often standing behind the chair of him of the blank face, sometimes shaking his fist at him, and sometimes looking pleasantly. Towards the end of the communications, she said that Blodge appeared in a new dress, consisting of a flowing purple robe, with a silver band around his waist, and a crown of gold upon his head.

"And now," continued the lady Medium, when Blodge had ceased communicating with the man of the blank face, "Now I see him (Blodge) retire into a beautiful arbor, which is filled with little children clothed in white. He holds a book in his hand, and is reading to the children. The place is full of other spirits also, and a lovely female, dressed in a flowing robe of white, stands among the children. She puts a sparkling jewel in the hand of each of the little ones, and sends them on a mission to earth, bidding them to return to her. And now the little white-robed children are in this room, running all about, and now they move away and return to the white-robed female who awaits them. In the hand of each, where just now sparkled the glittering jewel, there is now a lustreless bauble. The female spirit breathes upon the baubles, and immediately they change into bright and beautiful birds, which fly away."

The above concluded all the manifestations which occurred at the circle at the house of Mr. W. on the evening in question.

CHAPTER VIII.

POCAHONTAS AND OTHER INDIANS.

It was a dark muggy night; the heavens were black above, and the city lamps below gave no sign of light, because they had been put out by a city law, made after a Common Council almanac, which said that the moon would shine that night, and therefore it was not necessary for the city to go to the expense of lamplight when there would be moonlight ready made to hand. But the moon did not shine, according to Common Council calculation and economy, and therefore the citizens of New-York in general, and ourself in particular, were in the dark; and alone in the dark with the drizzling rain beating in our face, we walked down Chambers-street, through College-place and down Robinson-street, until we came to the residence of Mr. L. T. . Not a single person did we meet on the way, although it was only half-past nine o'clock. We looked around to see if we could discover a police star shining out in the darkness, but even this consolation was denied us; the police stars, like all other stars, had vanished, and if we had been murdered that night, we feel assured that the murderer would never have been discovered, unless some spirit witness should have made a manifestation next day. As, however, we were as usual on a spiritual tour we did not feel much afraid of being murdered, and with our coat only a little damaged by the wet, and our boots somewhat soiled, we entered the spiritual circle assembled at Mr. T.'s.

The two girl Mediums, whom we have before described, were present as usual, and the room was more crowded with inquirers and spectators than we had ever before seen it.

"Is there any spirit here who wishes to communicate with me?" said we, seating ourself at the table, and taking the hand of the youngest girl Medium. "If there is, please take possession of this Medium and make the communication."

The girl immediately began to twist and turn her body and move the muscles of her face, and finally snatching her hand from ours, struck it violently on the table several times, and then extended it back again to us. We clasped it and said:

"Does a spirit wish now to speak to us?"

The girl struck her hand, with ours in it, three times on the table, which, taking of course as an affirmative answer, we continued—

"Who is the spirit? Is it Oliver Blodge, who manifested himself last week at Mr. W.'s, when we were present?"

"No."

"Is it the Rev. John Maffit, who also has manifested himself in several circles where we have been present?"

"No."

"Who then is it? Will you spell out your name by alphabet?"

"Yes."

And the alphabet being called, we proceeded to put down the letters designated by the so-called spirit; but the result, after a few moments' steady work, was extremely complicated in the way of letters, and somewhat funny in the appearance the letters made. We have seen many hard-looking Dutch names written, and some Hottentot ones, which no one but a man with an immense flexibility of tongue, capacity of throat and strength of jaws would undertake to pronounce; but Dutch and Hottentot were nothing to words which the spirit now spread before us. There were three words to the sp-rit's name as spelt out, but we have room only for the last, which read, as near as we could make it out "Lotohotowosky."

"What nation do you belong to?" asked we despair ingly as we gazed on the name. "Are you Polish? for your name looks a little that way."

"No."

"Well, then we give it up. Please inform us, for we cannot guess."

"Indian," was the answer spelt out by alphabet.

"Did we ever know you?"

"Yes."

"You must be mistaken; we never *knew* any Indians, and all the Indians we ever *saw* were at Barnum's Museum, and of their being the real Simon Pure article certain waggish persons have expressed great doubt. They looked Indian, however, and whooped in the most approved style, and therefore we were satisfied; but, friend Lotohotowsky, we must say again that we never knew your Indianship.

"You did."

"Well, Lotohotowosky, how and where did we ever know you?"

"You talked English for me."

"Ah, this is news indeed; but although we have not the faintest idea where or when we ever talked English for you or any other Indian, you may have it your own way.. But tell us, if you please, what you want with us now."

"If you don't look out, I'll knock you on the head."

"Lotohotowosky, knock away—we are ready to receive any physical demonstration in proof of spiritualism."

But the knock was not given, and we continued—

"Lotohotowosky, will you knock us now?"

"No."

"Will you do it to night?"

"Yes."

"Here?"

"No."

"Will you do it when we walk up Robinson street?"

"No."

"When we walk up Chambers street?"

"No."

"When we go up Broadway?"

"Yes."

"When you knock us down in Broadway, will you leave us to take care of ourself?"

"No."

"Will you call a police officer?"

"No."

"Would one come if you did?"

"No."

"Do they ever come when they are wanted?"

"No."

"Lotohotowosky, you do not appear to think much of the New York police."

"Indian scare them all with a whoop."

The girl Medium here unloosed our hand, gave a slight shrug, recovered her natural state, and Lotohotowosky of course was gone. We ourself soon after departed.

We may state here, that all the answers of the supposed spirit of Lotohotowosky, to our questions, were spelt out by alphabet.

We voluntarily subjected ourself to the inconvenience and unpleasantness of walking up the whole length of Broadway, in order to give Lotohotowosky a chance to knock us down, and test the vigilance of the police, as he had represented it. But we reached home in safety, without the sign of a knock, either from the spirit of Lotohotowosky, or from the hand of a rowdy. We considered the last exemption more remarkable than the former.

A few evenings after the above occurrence, we were

present at a private circle where we found, among others, Mr. C., a Medium of our acquaintance, and the young lady Medium whom we described in our last week's report as being present at Mr. W.'s circle, and through whom the spirits not only spoke, but to whom they frequently made themselves visible. We have already given an account of the visions which this Medium saw when we were present at Mr. W.'s. On the evening above referred to, when we again met this seeing and speaking lady Medium, she looked very different from when we at first saw her. The same black and bright eyes were indeed there, but the bloom on her cheek had given way to an almost deadly paleness, which enhanced the brilliancy of her eyes, and gave her an unearthly expression which attracted the attention of all towards her. Her eyes seemed constantly fixed on vacancy, and when we extended our hand in greeting, and addressed her by the name of Josy (the familiar contraction of her right Christian name, Josephine,) she answered:

"Josy not here—gone away; Pocahontas here, and speak to you. Pocahontas know you, and glad to see you; but Josy gone away."

We turned a look of inquiry around the circle; we did not exactly understand the position of things, and wished for information. We were answered, that Josephine, the Medium, had for two days been possessed by the spirit of Pocahontas; that during that time she had not appeared or talked in her natural character, and that every question asked her, was answered as if Pocahontas was speaking through her.

"Pocahontas," said we, "do you talk Indian?"

"Pocahontas talk very good English; talk better soon."

"Can you give a war whoop, Pocahontas?"

Pocahontas gave a whoop which made us jump slightly. It takes a great deal to make us jump; but we must confess that Pocahontas's whoop was so good, that we were somewhat startled.

"Pocahontas, do you remember John Smith?"

"Yes, Pocahontas remember him; Pocahontas love him; Pocahontas love you all—do you much good."

A circle was now formed around the table, in which Pocahontas took a seat, laid her hands mechanically before her, still keeping her eyes fixed on vacancy.

"Do you see any spirits around us, Pocahontas?" asked one of the company.

"Yes, Pocahontas see myriads—the room is full."

"Is King Phillip or Massasoit here?" asked we.

"Powhatan is here," answered Pocahontas, "and he will soon make himself known."

At this moment, another young lady, with a pensive cast of countenance, whom we have noticed at various circles which we have visited, particularly at that of Mr. W., and who was also a Medium, rose from her chair, and commenced flapping her hands violently before the face of Mr. C.

The Medium with the pensive countenance continued to flap her hands before the face and over the head of

Mr. C. for at least fifteen minutes, without flagging in the least. During all this time Pocahontas kept her eyes steadily fixed on the motion of the hands of her of the pensive countenance, and when about fifteen minutes had elapsed, she suddenly exclaimed:

"That's right, Powhatan; do your duty."

"Then the person who is now flapping her hands before Mr. C. is possessed by the spirit of Powhatan?" asked we.

"Pocahontas sees Powhatan; he is here, and will do something," was the answer.

Taking it therefore for granted that it was the spirit of Powhatan who was flapping his hands through the person of her of the pensive countenance, over Mr. C., we waited to see what Powhatan would do, although we confess we were deeply in the fog as to what were his intentions.

Soon Mr. C. closed his eyes; then his whole frame became convulsed, and then instantly he fell over, chair and all, on the floor.

"Pocahontas, what is Powhatan doing with Mr. C.?" asked one of the company.

"Wait and you shall see," was the answer of Pocahontas.

We did wait, and we looked at Mr. C. extended on the floor, to all appearance dead, if it had not been for a slight twitching of his muscles, which convinced us that he was still alive.

"Perhaps he had better be taken care of," said some one.

"Powhatan will take care of him; let him lie," said Pocahontas.

And he was left, according to the directions of Pocahontas, with his head in the lap of Powhatan, or rather of the lady of the pensive countenance, through whom Powhatan was said to be operating.

Mr. C. laid thus for some ten minutes, when he suddenly rose up from the floor, gave his shoulders a shrug, and his eyes a convulsive opening, and leaning against the mantel-piece, he came to himself, wondering what the spirits had been doing with him. We of course did not know, and it is still a mystery what Powhatan was after.

The circle at the table, which had in some measure been broken up by the operations of Powhatan with Mr. C., was now resumed, and no sooner was such the case, than Pocahontas rose up, extended her hand towards a lady present, and said:

"Pocahontas will do you much good. You will accomplish what you will. You have a good heart, and God will bless you."

"Then I shall be the happiest of mortals," said the lady.

"It shall be so; Pocahontas has said it, and Pocahontas loves you—God loves you. You know what I mean; what I say, thrills through your soul. Aha! I know it. Bless you!"

Whatever it was that Pocahontas knew thrilled through the soul of the lady, we of course cannot tell; we only know that the lady appeared to understand

Pocahontas; that it seemed to touch a chord in her heart; for we saw a tear falling down her cheek.

After this there was a circle formed in the dark, to see if the spirits would manifest themselves through the medium of lights. We were of the number; but no lights came after a sitting of some half hour's duration. The spirits finally said, by raps, that the circle was not formed right, and on calling on the spirits for information as to who should and who should not be members of the circle, we found ourself among the number who had to leave. And so we departed.

A few evenings after the above manifestations, in company with the gentleman with the flaxen moustache and imperial, whom we have before mentioned, we started to go to the residence of Mr. W., in order to see whether the spirit of Pocahontas still kept possession of the lady with the dark hair and the bright eyes. On our way, however, we stopped at the hall in Broadway, near Eleventh-street, where the Spiritualists hold a conference every Tuesday evening.

We found the hall crowded, and a young man attempting to speak. He professed to be possessed by the spirit of Shakspeare, and although we could not recognize much of Shakspeare in his language or ideas, yet we felt convinced he was himself unconscious of what he was doing or saying, and that some influence beyond his control impelled him to speak. We believe that he could not have mustered courage enough to do it if he had been in his natural state, for he seemed extremely young, and not one who in his natural state could face an audience with a speech. The audience, however, seemed not inclined to hear him, and manifested their disinclination by hissings and other signs of their wish not to hear him.

All this was very wrong, especially for a body of professed spiritualists, who should, we think, listen to everything purporting to come from spirits. The issue of the matter was, that the young Medium talked away for some time amid much confusion, and then sat down.

The next person who stood up to address the audience, was the lady with the pensive countenance, whom we mentioned above as having been a few evenings previously possessed with the spirit of Powhatan. The spirit of Henry Clay was said now to possess her by entrancement. At least she announced herself as Henry Clay, and what she said, was mainly on the subject of spiritualism. The manner of her delivery was graceful and sometimes sublime. In the course of his speech, Henry Clay, through the lady, denounced the course which had been pursued by the audience with reference to the young man who had before spoken.

There was another speech made by another lady Medium named Mrs. F., who came, we believe, from Pittsburgh, and had already created some excitement among the spiritualists of New-York as a speaking Medium. What spirit animated her we did not learn, but she poured forth a stream of pretty words about spiritualism, but said nothing very tangible for us to chronicle.

After the conference had concluded its sitting, we proceeded with our friend with the flaxen moustache and imperial to the residence of Mr. W., where we found a crowded circle. Among others were the lady Medium, whom Pocahontas, as we before have said, had taken possession of, and the lady who had spoken at the conference in the character of Henry Clay. But the spirit of Pocahontas had departed from the one, and that of Henry Clay from the other, and both had resumed their natural characters.

In the centre of the table around which the circle was seated, there was a pretty bouquet of flowers, which had been presented by a gentleman to the lady Medium who had been the medium of the communications of Pocahontas. As soon as the circle had been formed, there was silence kept for the space of some moments, in order to produce harmony in the circle and give the spirits, if they so chose, an opportunity to manifest themselves. The silence was at length broken by the rising of a very interesting looking lady, with black hair and eyes, and a spiritual cast of countenance, who approached a gentleman of pale countenance and very large eyes, and commenced making passes before him with her hands. When the passes ceased, the gentleman opened his mouth and spoke. Most of what he said was on the theory of spiritualism, and as he spoke continually during the evening, to the exclusion of almost all other manifestations, and as we have not room enough to record half of what he said, we can only give the general purport. He spoke, successively, in the characters of Swedenborg, Shelly, Milton and Edmund Kean.

He said, in substance, that the great law of God was

love, and that the law of men should be love to one another; that the flowers on the table were emblematic of the purpose for which the circle had met that night—purity; that poisonous laurel was the wreath for the conqueror's brow, but that flowers were the wreaths for the pure. That the mission of spirits was to elevate mankind. That spirits sometimes assume other names than their own, assuming names well known in order to attract that attention which their own unknown names would fail to command, but that in such cases the names of others were assumed by the authority and with the knowledge of their rightful owners. He said also that a majority of the members of Congress were mere political tricksters, and that spiritualism would soon change for the better the complexion of that body. (We here mentally hoped that the gentleman might be right.) The gentleman Medium, with the large eyes, also gave an extract from one of Daniel Webster's speeches, and a recitation of a few lines from the soliloquy of Shakspeare's Hamlet, "To be or not to be." The soliloquy, as far as given, was not correct to the text, but it was very near. Perhaps Edmund Kean, who was supposed to be speaking, was rather rusty in the text, owing to his not having practised the histrionic art in the spirit world.

These speeches of the gentleman Medium having been finished, Pocahontas suddenly took possession of the lady whom she had before chosen. Elevating her hands and eyes to Heaven, she said:

"Pocahontas repeats what she has before said. Mortals know little of the beauty of angels. Pocahontas will give you each a flower. Josy (meaning herself does not like to break the bouquet, but Pocahontas says she must."

And kneeling down, Pocahontas (Josy) took the bouquet from the center of the table and reached it forth to the gentleman speaking-Medium, telling him that she gave him the center flower, which was a japonica.

The gentleman Medium thanked her, and spoke as if he was a young Indian who had known her in youth and wandered with her through the woods for the flowers. He also again made a few very pretty remarks on the emblematic language of flowers.

Pocahontas now told the gentleman Medium to separate the bouquet, reserving the japonica for himself. This was done, and Pocahontas, taking the japonica in her hands, raised it upwards and said:

"Thus fall away all earthly pleasures, (meaning the separation of the rest of the flowers from the japonica) leaving only hope."

She then gave back the flower to the gentleman Medium, shook hands with all in the circle, fell into her chair, gave a slight shiver, and Pocahontas had gone, and Josy was once more herself.

No other manifestations of any interest, occurred during this evening.

CHAPTER IX.

SPIRITUAL CONFERENCE, SPIRITUAL BELIEVERS, AND PICKLES.

We pause here, to rest a moment from our journeyings among the spiritual circles, and to indulge in a didactic rather than in a wonderful manifestation chapter.

We one evening took our way to Dodworth's Musical Hall, in Broadway, where the Spiritualists every Tuesday evening hold a conference. We found the Hall full—full of intellectual looking faces, mingled with many of a skeptical cast, and sprinkled with a goodly number of bright eyes and chiselled features of female beauty, where a mixture of mortal and spirit, gave the whole "form," as the spiritualists would say, a magnet of attraction which pulled hard upon our earthly organs of vision.

As we entered, a fine looking elderly gentleman, named Dr. Hallock, occupied the stand. The substance of his remarks was, that the subject of Spiritualism was one of grave import; that the object for which spiritualists met in that hall, was not so much for spiritual manifestations, as to relate facts in regard to Spiritualism, of which the relators had been witness, and thus build the foundations of this phenomena on a strata of truth which cannot be gainsayed. He referred to some manifestations which had taken place in the Hall at their last meeting, and while he did not doubt the honesty of the Mediums, he doubted their full development.

Dr. Hallock was followed by Dr. Gray, who appeared to us a thorough-going, but reasonable spiritualist. The purport of his remarks was that the world had been governed too long by authority; by king this and that, by that author and this author; that names were nothing, as long as truth, consonant with reason, was elicited; and that spirits in advanced stages of a Medium's development, never communicated by names.

Dr. Gray was succeeded by an old gentleman in a long coat, whose name we did not learn. He appeared from his broken accent, to be a foreigner, and gave evidence that in point of acuteness, his head was as long as his coat. He said that he did not like to be humbugged, and that he had been at a certain place a few evenings before, where he thought they were trying to humbug him. A person present pretended (as the speaker thought,) to be possessed with a spirit, and that the spirit was talking through him. "I just looked at him," said the speaker, "and I thought he opened his eyes and peeped a little around to see the effect of what he was saying produced. So I walked up to Mr. —— and said, 'Mr. —— that fellow is humbugging.'" The gentleman in the long coat and with the long head.

said much more in the same strain, and we came to the conclusion that although he was a firm spiritualist on reasonable grounds, he was not one over whose eyes the wool could be pulled to any great extent.

The old gentleman in the long coat was followed by Mr. Ira Davis, who made some interesting remarks on the subject of Spiritualism, and said what we were much pleased to hear. He said, in substance, that it would be well for spiritualists to put in practice the true principles of their theory, and unite in endeavoring to raise from false and unhappy positions those who were outcasts from society, simply because, although society said to them, "Why do you not change your position and adopt another course of life?" society did not make the first practical effort to help them to do so. Mr. Davis took the ground of expansive charity combined with material help, and called upon all spiritualists to practice with their pockets and hands what they preached with their mouths.

Thus much for the spiritual conference.

It is a fitting place here to record the result of our observations in reference to one particular phase of Spirit Rapping, viz: the different classes of believers which we have met at the various circles we have visited.

These classes are three—first, believers who always require a test; second, believers who style themselves "elevated," and will listen to nothing but what is spoken through speaking Mediums and clothed in the most flowery language; and third, believers who believe everything, and never stop to inquire whether there is reason in their belief or not.

We have seen the believers of all these three classes assembled at one table, and we have seen circles composed almost entirely of each. In all, the study has been curious.

And first of the Test Believers. These are generally very composed-looking individuals, who sit around the table with a calm, business-like air, which, while it inspires confidence, shows that anything wearing the least appearance of humbug, will not do.

"Is there any spirit here who wishes to communicate with me?" is the question which, after the manner of all other inquirers, these Test Believers ask. If the answer is "yes," they do not take it for granted that the spirit who answers, is the one which they wish, and which the spirit represents itself to be.

"Give me your signal knock," (or tip, as the case may be, according to whether it was a wrapping or tipping Medium,) is the answer which we have often heard by these test inquirers. If the signal rap or tip was given, or any other manifestation, by which the inquirer could identify the spirit, was afforded, it was well, and the inquirer was satisfied; but if not, the inquirer folded his arms and said he was not satisfied, and we think he was right.

The second class of believers we have styled, as they style themselves, "elevated." They are so elevated that they do not wish to listen to any communications, except those which purport to come from those who while "in the form" (as the spiritualists say) bore great names, such as Shakspeare, Swedenborg, Milton, Daniel Webster, Henry Clay, and a host of other names of the like calibre. Guardian spirits of those loved on earth are forgotten, and no spirit will be listened to, except it comes under an imposing name, and announces itself in a beautiful rigmarole of words. We have been present evening after evening when such communications were made through speaking Mediums, and we have watched the impression which those communications made on "elevated believers." "Did ever such language fall from mortal lips," has been the enthusiastic exclamation which we have heard a hundred times.

Last of all comes the third class, who believe everything. We have seen this class at a spiritual circle.

"Is the spirit of my little daughter here?" says a mother, bending over the table with folded hands, and the tears trickling down from her eyes. "Yes," is the answer, and the tears flow afresh, and the head is bowed with a deeper reverence. And then follows a long communication from daughter to mother, during which the tears are changed into sobs. We confess we sympathize with such parental feelings, whatever our opinion of the spirit answers may be.

"Is the spirit of my wife here?" asks another, and gray hairs are on the brow and wrinkles on the cheek of the inquirer. "Yes," is the answer, and then follow communications, which cause the wrinkles to be less apparent, and the face of the questioner lights up with joy. We sympathize with the feelings of this class of questioners also.

"Is there any spirit which wishes to communicate with me?" asks another, and no matter what spirit comes up, the inquirer is satisfied.

In reference to such an inquirer we have a fact to record, which we were told by the inquirer himself.

"Is there *any* spirit who wishes to communicate with me?" said one of these extremely credulous believers, while seated in a circle and waiting for any manifestation which might take place.

"Yes," was the answer, and the supposed spirit spelt out by the alphabet, the name of "Pickles."

"Well, who is Pickles?" said one, and ha! ha! laughed another.

But the sober inquirer and unhesitating believer answers:

"Never you mind about 'Pickles;' it is all right. Pickles means something, and we shall one day find out what it means."

"And now," said this believer in the spirit of "Pickles," appealing to us, in a conversation which we afterwards held with him, "what do you think—I have found out what 'Pickles' is."

"You don't say so! who is he?"

"Look at that," was the answer, and the believer in the spirit of "Pickles," handed us a letter.

We looked at the letter; but the writing was awful, and it covered four sides of a letter sheet closely written.

"Why, it is signed with the name of 'Mungo Park,'" said we.

"Of course it is," said the unwavering believer, "and it explains all about 'Pickles;' just as I said—'Pickles' has turned up right."

We endeavored to read the letter, in order to find out who "Pickles" was; but the whole letter was hieroglyphics to us, and we gave it up in despair.

"Let me read it for you," said the unwavering believer.

He read it, and the purport of it was that Mungo Park had discovered, in the interior of Africa, a strange plant, called in the Arabic or some other language, "Bickles," which the unwavering believer interpreted "Pickles."

Mungo Park, in his letter, said that this plant Biccles or Pickles, was of rare virtue, and that the unwavering believer would be made the medium of making its virtues known to the world. Whether he was to go into the interior of Africa to accomplish this result, the letter did not state, and the unwavering believer is still in the city of New York.

"Where did you get this letter of Mungo Park?" said we.

"Through the post-office," was the answer.

At this point of the conversation, we suddenly separated from the believer in "Pickles;" but we have since learned from him, that two pails of pickles were actually delivered at his feet, by some unknown person, who he declares was sent by the spirits.

CHAPTER X.

THE SPHERES OF THE SPIRIT WORLD—THE LOWER, OR INFERNAL SPHERE.

One evening we found ourself in the midst of a private circle of Spiritualists, to which we had been invited some time previously. The company present was very large; so numerous that not one half could sit at the table, which was a larger one than we have been in the habit of seeing at the various places which we have visited.

The Medium present was a young girl, apparently not above eighteen years of age. Her hair was black, parted simply over her forehead. Her face was full and round; the bloom of health was on her cheeks, and a beautiful pair of black eyes looked timidly out at those by whom she was surrounded. Her hands were small and well formed, and as they rested on the table, we confessed to ourself that we had seldom seen a more perfect model of a female hand, cast in a mould of beauty, with a well-rounded palm and tapering fingers. She sat perfectly passive, and waited with those around her for the manifestation of whatever spirit should choose to make known its presence.

"Let the spirits take their own way," said the gentleman at whose house we were a visitor, "and we shall get better communications."

We, of course had no objections to the spirits doing just exactly as they pleased, and while we were waiting for them to do something, we cast our eyes around the circle to take a note of the persons who composed it.

All the persons about us had the appearance of firm believers and sincere-hearted individuals. They did not belong to the aristocracy of New York; but they belonged to that worthy middle class which every country should cherish; for they were of the number of the working and producing citizens with whom honesty and truth are virtues to be loved for themselves alone, and with whom labor is a thing which brings self-respect and public honor.

One individual, however, alone of the circle, struck us in such a light as to occasion particular remark in this chapter. And he drew our attention, from the interest which he manifested in the subject of spiritualism, and the reasonable light in which, although he appeared to be a firm believer, he viewed the whole phenomena as we would say, and the spiritual manifestations, as the spiritualists would call them.

The face of the individual in question was encircled and adorned with an immense pair of, what is called, sandy-colored whiskers; his hair was of the same hue; his face pale, but he possessed a pair of gray, little, twinkling eyes, which kept moving around the circle as if he knew what he was about, and which we thought, displayed a remarkable degree of intelligence. He was dressed in a gray sack-coat, gray vest and gray pantaloons. Whether or not he was partial to gray spirits, such as Shakspeare mentions, we know not, but certain it is that this gentleman in gray was, to use a modern classical expression, "around" in the way of Spiritualism.

The circle waited some time for spiritual manifestations, and the man in gray cloth and with sandy whiskers, spread his hands reverently on the table and waited patiently with the rest.

But the spirits would not come. At length the man in gray threw back his head, and commenced singing a plaintive song of a spiritual character. There was a deep silence, and we expected some very sober spirit would have presented itself, but there came instead one who announced himself through the girl Medium in a rich brogue, which left no doubt but that while on earth, his home in the early part of his life, at least, had been the green isle of Erin.

"Faith, and how are you? Here I am sure, come to see you," said the supposed spirit of the Irishman, through the mouth of the girl Medium.

"How do you do, friend; but who are you addressing?" answered a fat little man, with an apple face and a pair of small steel spectacles stretched across the top of it. The fat little man had not spoken before, and had been so quiet in every way that we had not noticed him. We are under the impression that he had not much faith in spirits, although he looked as if his faith in the existence of markets, was lively and not to be argued out of him.

"Faith, I came to see ye all," was the Irish spirit's answer to the fat little man with the apple face.

A long desultory conversation here followed between the spirit of the Irishman and various persons around the table, during which the spirit of the Irishman maintained the proverbial wit of his race. He also gave his name, which was one of those very common among the Irish people, but which did not identify him to any of those present, as no one of the circle had ever known him on earth. It is not in accordance with our views to give the whole of this conversation; the majority of it was mere pleasant badinage between the spirit and the man in gray and the man with the apple face. We shall only give that part of it which bears directly on the subject of spiritualism, which we are investigating.

"Patrick, (his first name was Patrick) Patrick, how did you get in the room?" said the man in gray.

"I came in with the atmosphere, sure; popped in when the door was open."

"But I have not seen that it was open when you came in, or even for some time before," answered the man in gray.

"Sure it has been open to-night, hasn't it, boss; and what was to hinder me from coming in thin?"

"Well, Patrick, how will you get out?"

"Faith, the same way I come in; do you hear that, boss?"

"Yes, I hear it; but suppose the door is not opened;

how then, Patrick, will you manage it?" and the man in gray leaned back, as if he thought he had asked Patrick a clincher.

"The door 'll be opened, boss, sure; for some of ye will be afther going out, and thin I'll go out, too."

The man in gray looked at the man with the apple face, and the man with the apple face looked back at the man in gray, and apple remarked to gray that he did not think Patrick was very clear on the subject of the entrance and exit of spirits.

"Patrick, what sphere are you in?" asked apple-face.

"It's the sixth sphere, sure, that I'm in, boss."

"What kind of place is Heaven, Patrick?"

"It's a beautiful place, boss, and ye'll be a happy man if ye get there. Pray to the Lord, boss, and may be ye'll get in."

"What sort of a place, Patrick, is the first sphere of the spirit world?"

"They're not happy, a bit, boss; they want something which they cannot get."

"How is the second sphere?"

"Jist a little better, boss."

"How is the third sphere?"

"They're trying to put up a bit, boss."

"How is the fourth sphere?"

"Not quite so bad, boss; pray to the Lord, boss; love the Lord, boss."

"How the fifth?"

"Middling good, boss; but not so good as it might be; pray to the Lord, boss."

"How the sixth?"

"That's where I am, boss."

And Patrick here ceased his communications about the spheres.

"Patrick," continued the man with the apple face, "do you see any spirit around me?"

"Yes, sure, boss; there's one standing behind your chair."

"What does he look like, Patrick?"

"Faith, and he don't look as if he was much; he's got a long black gown on, and he holds his head down, so that I can't see his face, boss."

"Ask him what his name is, Patrick."

"There now," said the supposed spirit of Patrick, speaking through the girl Medium, who looked at the back of the chair on which the man with the apple face sat, and seemed to be addressing the invisible spirit there stationed,—"there now, d'ye hear what the gintleman says? he wants to know your name; hould up your head then and tell it like a man; sure you're not afraid to let the gintleman know your name."

But the spirit with the black gown and hang-down head, whom Patrick said he saw standing behind the chair of the fat man with the apple face, refused to give his name.

And then there followed from the Irish spirit a long series of commands and requests to the spirit with the black gown, that he would tell his name, and if he wasn't "ashamed of himself," make known who he was.

The whole resulted in the announcement by Patrick,

that the black gown had finally said that he had been, while in the form, (that is, when he lived on earth,) a certain clergyman who had been quite famous. But the man with the apple-face requiring some test that the black gown was the spirit of the clergyman whom he professed to be, Patrick said that he (the black gown) still kept his head down, and would give no test, and the man with the apple-face then said that the black gown might go; for if he was a spirit at all, he was a bad and lying spirit.

This latter remark of the man with the apple-face, led to a short argument, or rather interchange of ideas between him and the gentleman in gray, on the subject of requiring tests from spirits, in order that the inquirer might know whether the spirit with whom he was talking, was or was not the one which that spirit represented itself to be.

The man with the apple-face contended strongly that tests in all cases should be required; "for," said he, "even spiritualists say that spirits are continually coming up, assuming names which do not belong to them, and often telling up and down lies. Now, I do not understand such a course of proceeding on the part of the inhabitants of the spirit world. If they are permitted to cut such capers, it strikes me that the spirit world is a very queer place, and not much better than this world, where we expect to hear about one hundred lies to one truth. No, sir, if a spirit wishes to communicate with me, he must identify himself, if he professes to be one whom I have known on earth; and if he is a stranger, he must tell me something that I don't know, and not give me a long rigmarole of fine words. If a spirit can speak ten or fifteen minutes in a rigmarole of fine words about flowers, and the beauty of heaven, and the future triumph of spiritualism, that spirit can give me some test that it is a spirit. I require a test, sir; I would not take for law and gospel, suck in, if I may so express myself, all a supposed spirit told me, without it agreed with the reason and common sense which God Almighty has given me; or without it made it plain that it was not a mortal, but a spirit from the other world that spoke. I have seen much of this latter phase of drinking in pretty words, and taking them as the language of immortals. I have seen circles sit with open mouths and ears, listening to a rigmarole of words, and exclaiming that it could not come from mortal lips, when at the same time I have heard and read language twice as beautiful, and ten times as reasonable in sentiment and philosophy, from nothing but mortals. But if you were to place this handsome and more reasonable language and sentiment of mortals before these blind disciples of spiritualism, they would hoot at it. I require tests, sir, and tests I must have."

A spirit now spoke through the Medium, announcing himself as William Scott, who professed to have known the gentleman of the house where the circle of which we were the visitor, was formed. When asked where he knew him, he answered that he knew him at the diggings in California, at St. Mary's; that he (William Scott,) died in crossing the Isthmus, and that he belonged to Liverpool.

The gentleman of the house, after some reflection, said that he thought he recollected Scott in California; but the spirit of William Scott departed without making any further communication.

The spirit of Scott having taken his leave, the girl Medium was for some moments in a state of quiescence.

Soon, however, her hand began to slap on the table violently, and her frame to be violently contorted. Then she sobbed and groaned, and appeared altogether in great distress.

The general opinion around the table, among the spiritualists, was that she was possessed by an undeveloped spirit, and some one suggested that a few passages out of the Bible should be read.

The man with the apple face complied with this suggestion, and having opened at random to the part of the New Testament which speaks of the raising of Lazarus from the grave, read a few verses relative to that subject.

The Medium gradually became more quiet, and at length broke out into a sort of prayer, the purport of which was, that God would banish the evil influence then around the circle. The prayer was long and earnest, and while the Medium gave utterance to it, the tears rolled down her cheeks like rain.

"Who is this spirit?" was the question asked by some one of the circle.

"Shadrach Smith," was the answer; "and I have never communicated with mortals before."

"Who is Shadrach Smith?" was the question asked by the man with the apple face.

"He is the father of the Medium," said the gentleman of the house.

The girl Medium now suddenly jumped from the table, ran to the corner of the room, and shading her face with her hands, exclaimed:

"What a funny place I see! it can't be that any one lives here; what a funny little place—oh! oh!"

Then suddenly she became violently agitated, and casting up her hands, as if to express her horror, she screamed in a voice which affected the whole circle:

"Oh, dear! oh, dear! it is the place where the bad spirits live. I am right among them; oh, dear! oh! oh! oh!" and the Medium shrank into the corner of the room, making violent motions with her hand, as if she would repel the advance of something horrible to look at. Then she continued:

"Oh! oh! oh! I never knew a thing that had but one head; it has seven heads; it will bite me; it will stick its great horns in me! Oh, what horns! Why did they send me here in this awful place? What have I done that I should be sent here?"

And again the girl Medium shrieked and screamed, and continued so to do, until suddenly she came out of her trance, and then with tears and sobs, she threw herself into the arms of some one of her female friends, exclaiming—

"Oh! it is horrible; I will never have anything more to do with spirits."

"What is the meaning of all this?" asked the man with the apple face.

"The spirit of Isaiah has often been up here," said the gentleman of the house, "and has promised to show this Medium awful sights if she did not believe. I presume he has now shown her some of the mysteries of the lower spheres into which those who have been bad on earth at first pass—the region, as we say, of undeveloped spirits."

The man with the apple face made no answer, but soon left, and we went with him.

This is a faithful record of what we witnessed at the above private circle.

CHAPTER XI.

THE DREAM SPIRIT.

The following occurred at a strictly private circle, consisting of four persons, who were all Mediums, and whom we shall designate as Mediums Numbers 1, 2, 3 and 4.

As soon as the four Mediums had taken their places, the question was asked by each one in succession, "Is there a spirit here who wishes to communicate with me?" The table tipped an affirmative answer to Medium No. 2.

It was then requested that the spirit would give its name, and, in order to avoid the trouble of the alphabet, several names were written upon slips of paper and put on the table. The papers were picked up consecutively by No. 2, but no response was rendered. A discussion then arose as to what it could mean, the spirit having said it would point out its name.

"Is the name amongst those written?"

"Yes."

It was then suggested that perhaps the spirit was desirous that some one else, and not No. 2, should pick out the papers with the names written on them. This suggestion was adopted: No. 1 shut his eyes, and took up the papers singly, until the table tipped thrice, (yes,) meaning that the paper which No. 1 at that moment held in his hand was the right one.

The paper was then opened, and the name "George" was found to be the one written within.

"It is your cousin," said Medium No. 1, addressing Medium No. 2.

Medium No. 2 answered, "It cannot be my cousin George, for he is alive."

Medium No. 1, addressing the supposed spirit: "Is the name and relationship correct? Are you, as No. 2 has said, still alive?"

The table, in answer, tipped three times, meaning "Yes."

No. 2 shook his head in doubt; the alleged fact that the spirit of his live cousin was there and wished to communicate with him, was rather a puzzler even for so firm a believer as he was.

"Perhaps," said Medium No. 1, addressing Medium No. 2, "perhaps the spirit of your cousin has left the form (body) and came here to visit you while his form or body is asleep."

The question as to the correctness of this supposition on the part of Medium No. 1 was then put to the table, and the answer, returned by taps, was that the supposition was correct.

"Are you in the spirit world?"

The table tipped twice, by which it was understood that the spirit intended to answer "partially."

No. 1.—"Do you mean to say that you are of the spirit world while absent from the body?"

"Yes."

No. 1.—"You are not dead?"

"No."

No. 2.—"You are in a dream?"

"As you would say in a dream."

This latter answer was written through the hand of one of the Mediums present.

"You mean," said Medium No. 1, "that we call it a dream, but that you are positively present?"

"Yes."

"Well, I don't understand this," said No. 2; "I never heard of such a circumstance before. How can the spirit be here and the body still alive?"

"Is there any mistake?" said Medium No. 1, addressing the spirit.

"No."

No. 1.—"You are deceiving us?"

"No."

"Let us test it," said the Medium No. 4.

This suggestion was adopted. The names of several places were then written, and when London, which was among them, was pointed out by one of the Mediums, the spirit indicated that that was the correct place.

The occupation of the spirit was then asked, but in this the answer was not correct, as it had been in the case of residence.

On inquiring the reason, the following answer was written through the hand of Medium No. 1:

"Is it for want of harmony, and because of the doubt existing, which makes the power to communicate difficult."

No. 2—"I admit I was not in harmony; the appearance of the spirit of a living friend is so extraordinary that I feel quite at fault with it."

"Will you write through one of us the reason why you come here?"

"Yes."

The following communication from the spirit was then written through the hand of Medium No. 1:

"Do you not know that the spirit is the same, whether in the form or out of the form? Do you wonder that the spirit should be governed by its affinity—that it should seek it? You know how I loved you even in the pleasant days of childhood; and now in our prime I have desired, you know little how I have desired to be with you before; and now only has it been permitted me to accomplish that which has been for some time my earnest wish. I am with you, and you——"

Here the medium's arms became so heavy that he was alarmed, and he endeavored to lift his arm with the other hand, his countenance at the same time exhibiting an expression of pain. Medium No. 2 not observing the pain, but seeing the awkward effort of No. 1 to lift his arm began to laugh, when No. 1 implored him for God's sake not to do so. At this moment the pressure of heaviness on the arm of No. 1 ceased, and with it his writing. The sentence of the spirit communication was finished by impression (as the spiritualists say) as follows:

"And you will not receive me, but doubt my presence."

No. 4 again suggested the test as to the name. This was acceded to, and No. 1, with closed eyes, picked out the same name several times in succession. A conversation then ensued as to the singularity of the circumstance, when it was proposed that the same test should again be tried. It was then observed that one of the papers were missing; the question was proposed whether the name was amongst those remaining.

"No."

The papers were then all opened, and the name George was not found among them.

Search was then made and at last the missing paper was found in the hat of No. 2.

"Is this the name?" said Medium No. 2, holding up the missing paper.

"Yes."

"Will you communicate to me the impression you have received to-night?"

"Perhaps." This answer was given by two tips of the table.

"Will you be impressed to convey to me when you write such intelligence as shall make me know that it is really you who are present?"

"Yes, if possible."

Medium No. 1 then spoke to a spirit who had been

communicating with him, and asked if she saw the spirit of George.

"Yes."

"Will you impress him to remember that which he has seen to-night, when he awakes out of his dreams?"

"Yes."

"How? Will it be in the nature of a dream?"

"Yes."

Medium No. 2.—"Shall we hear from him (George) to this effect?"

"Yes."

"You are not deceiving me?"

"No."

"If you are truthful, you will touch me."

And Medium No. 1 was touched immediately on both hands, at least so he said, and the touch continued while the following questions were propounded:

"You are touching me?"

"Yes."

"You know where?"

"Yes."

"Will you answer where?"

"Yes."

"On my head!"

"No."

"Mouth?"

"No."

"On my face?"

"No."

"On my hands?"

"Yes."

"The answer," said Medium No. 1, "is correct, the sensation I experienced was as though some person had lightly spread a hand over both of my hands."

The circle now broke up, and the several members remarked that they should look for a letter from "George" in London, confirming the fact, as they think, that while his body was asleep in London, his spirit was here in New-York with his cousin and the circle above referred to.

CHAPTER XII.

SPIRITUAL HUSBANDS.

We were present one evening at a private spiritual circle composed of some ten persons. The manifestations (as they are called) which took place, were among the most curious that we have collected for our spiritual budget.

When the circle had been formed, and we had time to take a glance at those who surrounded us, two persons of the number particularly attracted our attention. The one was a young man slight in person, with large dreamy eyes which he kept devoutly fixed with an abstracted gaze on the table before him, as if he expected every moment a spirit would start out from it to greet his sight—he was evidently the firmest kind of a believer. The other was a short, stout man, of middle age, with a keen eye, and a face on which "don't believe it" was written as plain as if the letters had been stamped in the flesh.

All those around the table, as usual in such cases, asked in succession if there were any spirits there who wished to communicate with them; but the table gave no response, until the man with the large dreamy eyes, in a low, reverential voice, inquired whether the spirit of any one of his friends was present.

The table in answer, immediately gave the three usual tips to express an affirmative.

"Do you desire to talk with me?"

"Yes."

"Can you tell me your name?"

"Yes;" and the alphabet having been called by successive tips of the table, the letters "K. A. T. E." were those designated by tips of the table, when the man with the dreamy eyes pointed his finger through the alphabet, as the letters which formed the Christian name of the spirit.

"Will you tell me, if I point on the alphabet, the initial of your surname?"

"Yes."

The gentleman with the dreamy eyes again pointed to the different letters of the alphabet, until he came to K, when the table tipped, meaning thereby to say that K. was the initial of the spirit's surname.

"When in the form, were you married, as we would say?"

"Yes."

"How many times?"

"Twice."

"Well, what was your husband's name?"

A certain Christian name was then spelled out by the alphabet, which Christian name the spirit professed was that of the first husband.

The man with the dreamy eyes opened his organs of

vision a slight degree wider, and said that, as he did not know the Christian name of the spirit's first husband, he could not, of course, tell whether or not it was correct. But he knew the surname, and would therefore ask the spirit the initial of that. He accordingly put the question, and the initial was given by the spirit through the alphabet.

The man with the dreamy eyes now asked the name of the spirit's second husband, which was spelled out by alphabet, and the man with the dreamy eyes said the answers were correct. The circle being a private one, it is not proper for us to give the names as we heard them.

The man with the dreamy eyes now asked, we thought with a slight anxiety of face:

"Is either one of these persons who were your husbands on earth, according to the marriage rites of this world, your spiritual husband according to the laws or customs of the spirit world?"

"No."

"Have you a spiritual husband, and do you often go to him in order to be present with and around him?"

"Yes."

"Does the relation of husband and wife exist in the spirit world?"

"Yes."

"How—through affinity?"

"Yes."

"It does not then follow that they who are married

in the flesh, or in this world, are also married spiritually?"

"No."

"Is your spiritual husband with you in the spirit world?"

"No."

"Do you know the name of your spiritual husband? if so, tell its name."

The initials of the man with the dreamy eyes was then given by the supposed spirit, by means of the alphabet.

A sublime smile irradiated for a moment the countenance of the man with the dreamy eyes, as if he had been for some time longing to be the spiritual husband of the spirit now present, and as if he was now sublimely content with the announcement that he was indeed what he wished to be.

"Did you," said he, "write the piece of poetry to me commencing thus:

"I knew thee on earth; I loved thee then,
But now more dear to me:
Death can not sever the bond of love—
It cannot through eternity.
Hasten! oh, haste! for I would have
Thy spirit freed from clay:
Hasten! oh, haste! I yearn for thee
In everlasting day."

The table tipped emphatically, as much as to say that the spirit had most certainly written the above piece of poetry to the man with the dreamy eyes. We did not learn how the spirit wrote the said piece of poetry to the man with the dreamy eyes; but we presume it was either by way of impression, as the spiritualists say, or through the hand of some writing Medium. It matters not, however, which it was, so long as the man with the dreamy eyes believed it to be a simon pure article, and that he did so believe it, was evident from the profound air of reverence with which he received the communication of the spirit to that effect. But although satisfied that the consolatory stanzas came direct from the spirit, the man with the dreamy eyes seemed to wish for some additional information; for he asked:

"Is this piece of poetry which you sent me, truth?"

"Yes."

"Do you ever deceive me?"

"No."

The man with the dreamy eyes seemed now to be perfectly satisfied as far as it regarded both the poetry, the truth of it, and all else that related to his being the spiritual husband of the spirit.

As for ourself, we listened very attentively to the whole colloquy on the spiritual husband mystery, and we could not help drawing a comparison between the male Mormons of this world and the female spirits of the spirit land. We may have been irreverent; but we could not help it. Utah in this world, with one man surrounded with a bevy of wives, and the spiritual land with one woman in the middle of a bevy of husbands, seemed to rise before us, and we had mixed them up in strange confusion, when we were roused from our revery by the voice of the man with the dreamy eyes, who asked the spirit the question:

"Have you seen God?"

"No."

"What sphere are you in?"

"The seventh."

"You mean that you have not seen God personally?"

"Yes."

"But you have witnessed God's doings, have you not?"

"Yes."

"Have you seen Christ?"

"Yes."

"Was the spirit of Christ the spirit of God?"

"Yes."

"Is the spirit of Christ the same as man's spirit?"

The table tipped twice, by which the spirit meant to answer "partially."

"Do you mean that man's spirit is an emanation from God?"

"Yes."

"Were Christ's teachings truth?"

"Yes."

"Do you mean as man translates them to the letter?"

"No."

"In the spirit?"

"Yes."

The spirit who had chosen the man with the dreamy eyes for her spiritual husband, now bid "good night" to the circle, by means of the alphabet, and the man with the dreamy eyes could get no further communication from her. He seemed, however, to be in a state of ecstatic content with what he had received.

The little man with the keen eye, and whose face betokened that he was a skeptic in Spiritual Rappings, now said:

"I should like to see this table tipped up instead of down, as it has been all the evening."

No sooner said than done; for the table immediately tipped up instead of down.

The little man then said that he wished the table would tip on each of its sides successively.

The table complied with the little man's request, and tipped up on each of its sides in succession, and the little man leaned back in his chair, as if he were in some slight degree in a mist of wonder.

CHAPTER XIII.

THE CIRCLE IN THE PARLOR—THE CIRCLE IN THE ATTIC.

Having been informed that Miss K. F., a celebrated public rapping Medium, was in the city, and ready to receive visits from those desiring to investigate the subject of Spiritual Rappings, we of course made it a point to call upon her.

The room in which Miss K. F. received us, was a good sized parlor, splendidly furnished, with figured silk curtains, carved rosewood arm-chairs, rich carpet, and a large highly polished and square mahogany table in the centre.

At the head of the table sat the Medium, Miss F. herself, and the seats at the table were occupied by some fifteen ladies and gentlemen, all evidently, from their dress and manners, belonging to the upper and wealthy ranks of society.

Miss F. seems very young, and her claim to beauty cannot be disputed. Her hair, which is black as the wing of a raven, was parted in two simple curls, after the Madona style, giving striking effect to a fair forehead of an intellectual character, although not very high or expansive. Her eyes, like her hair, are of the

"No, not now, we used to have, but the manifestations have latterly much changed in their character. We have now, as a general thing, only raps."

Another gentleman now took the alphabet card in his hand, and asked if the spirit who professed to be ready to communicate with him would spell out the name he wished. The table rapped yes, and the gentleman pointed over the card with his pencil until the table had wrapped to a number of letters, which the gentleman said formed the correct name of which he was thinking.

This process of spelling out names by the alphabet formed the main part of the manifestations of the evening. Some of the inquirers said that the names they sought had been designated correctly by the raps, and others said that their answers were altogether incorrect. The correct and incorrect were about equally divided.

Last of all, we took our seat at the table, and asked that our name should be spelt out. The supposed spirit treated us very badly, mixing up its raps in strange confusion and giving us only a few letters correctly. We took occasion to rebuke slightly the spirit, and to request it if it could not tell the truth, not to say anything, and our communication ceased.

After this, Miss F. proceeded to show that the spirits at her call would rap in any part of the room. They did so rap on the floor, on each of the doors, and if we recollect right, one or two of the chairs.

Passing up Broadway a few evenings after our visit to the parlor circle of Miss F., we were attracted by a brilliant transparency, jutting on the sidewalk not far from the Broadway theatre. At first sight, we thought it was simply a gas announcement that oysters were behind or under the light, or that some new Barnum had entered the field of extraordinary curiosities, either in the animal, vegetable or human line, and we were about to pass on without particular investigation, when the words "Spiritual Manifestations," in very lengthy black letters, caught our eye, and we of course stopped. Our stoppage was a moment afterwards followed by our ascent up several long flights of steps until we thought we must be near the top of the building. We found at the door, which announced that we had come to the end of our journey, a little man with Judge Edmonds' work on spiritualism before him, and a box of small change beside him, which seemed as if it was gaping for more. We contributed twenty-five cents towards its further bulk, and entered.

We found ourself in a very small room, looking very much like an attic apartment, plainly furnished, with a black walnut table in the center, at which was seated a young girl. The sides of the room, in the rear of the table, were lined with females, while two or three gentlemen occupied as many chairs in front. The girl Medium was plain in appearance, but had a pleasant smile on her countenance, as if she felt very happy to aid all investigators into spiritual rapping mysteries.

A very bulky man, with light complexion and hair, and a very positive manner about him, took his seat at the table and asked for a spirit.

The table immediately slammed up and down, as if the spirit meant to say, that it was not only there, but determined to be heard.

The bulky man then inquired who it was, calling over at the same time various degrees of relationship, in none of which he found the spirit claimed to be. The spirit at length announced himself by violent tips of the table, as seemingly a friend, and the tips also designated the right name among a number of others which the bulky gentleman wrote down on a slip of paper. The bulky gentleman also found out in the same manner when his friend had died.

"Now, then," said the bulky gentleman, "if you are the spirit of my friend, you can give me a test; give me the telegraphic signal, by writing through the medium."

But the telegraph wires, this time refused to work; all communication was suddenly cut off, and the bulky gentleman was nonplused.

By this question of the bulky gentleman, we presumed that he either was or had been an operator in a telegraph office, and that his friend had been the same. The signal would have been an excellent test for the spirit friend to give; but it was not given.

Several other persons asked questions, and although the table in the attic tipped with extraordinary vigor, nothing satisfactory was obtained by the questioners.

A gentleman present, noticing that the table always tipped one way, (towards the Medium,) asked it to tip in an opposite direction. It slammed, in answer, every way.

This was all that occurred during our visit to the circle in the attic.

CHAPTER XIV.

FAMILY RAPS.

On a very cold evening, when we were somewhat fearful that the keenness of the air might freeze the spirits, we again visited the rooms of Mrs. B. The table was fully surrounded. Two members of the circle particularly attracted our attention. One was a round little man, with thin black hair, black mustaches and whiskers. The other was an elderly gentleman, with hair white as the snow, and a serious, reverent air, which told that he was an old and firm believer in spiritualism. The round little man was evidently a novice in spiritualism, and neither believed nor disbelieved what he knew nothing about.

"What shall I do—how shall I begin?" said the round little man, turning a slip of paper in one hand and a pencil in the other.

"Ask if there is a spirit here who wishes to communicate with you," said Mrs. B. very pleasantly, and endeavoring all she could to help him along.

The question was asked by the round little man, and three very loud raps on the table informed him that one from the spirit world, or at least the raps, were ready to talk to him.

"Now write down several names and point to them, and the spirit will probably rap at the right one," said Mrs. B.

The round little man complied, and finally found out that the spirit professed to be that of his father.

He asked several questions of his father as to what was his (the gentleman's) name, and also what business he followed. The name was not indicated aright by the raps, while as to his (the gentleman's) business or profession, the raps informed him that he was a broker. This the round little man said was no such thing, and rather repudiated all connection with brokers.

The next gentleman who questioned the supposed spirits, was a middle-aged person, with something of the air of an old bachelor about him. He desired some information respecting a lady recently married; but the information was not forthcoming—the spirits on that head were not communicative.

The next questioner received the following communication, spelt out by the alphabet, which was called by Mrs. B.

"I have visited you in circles, but have found it difficult to converse with you. I want to make my influence felt when you are engaged in important matters. The time is coming when you will confront the deriding coward—for skeptic he is not—with unflinching boldness, when the enraged bigots will brow-beat you for investigating a subject which so much conflicts with their prejudices."

The receiver of the above communication desired the

spirit who professed to send it, to spell out its name; but the spirit, or rather the raps, refused to do so, and the questioner, with the air of one who did not exactly know how the communication applied to him, said he had finished his inquiries.

The elderly man, with the snow white hair and reverent demeanor, now said:

"Daughter, father, grandfather, and sister, if you are all here, I wish you would unite in a communication to me; will you do so?"

A jumble of raps, all of different degrees of force, but given at the same time, was the answer which the elderly gentleman received. Then three single raps were given, and afterwards the following communication to the elderly gentleman, was spelt out by alphabet:

"Dear Father—I come first. Grandmother says the least shall be the greatest."

The name to this communication was also spelt out; but it is not appropriate that we should publish it.

This communication was no sooner finished, than the alphabet was again called for, and the elderly gentleman received another communication, as follows:

"Dear Brother—E. has delivered her message; tell H. her sister is progressing very fast, and she must try to keep pace with her, so that she can be able to enter her class in heaven."

This also was signed by the correct name.

This also was followed by another communication, as follows:

"Dear Grandson—I delight to linger near you, and

listen to your conversation. You are advancing rapidly to this knowledge, which will serve you in after life, and fit you for an elevated sphere in heaven."

This also was signed by a name, and was followed by the following:

"Dear Son—I love you and yours, and we shall all meet and know each other in heaven. Amen."

To the latter part of this communication, the same jumble of raps responded as they did to the first question of the elderly gentleman.

The elderly gentleman now seemed supremely happy that he had thus had an united communication from the spirits of his family in the spirit land. He asked no more questions, but remarked that during all the time the communications had been coming, he felt himself touched by the spirits who gave them.

Many other questions were asked by other members of the circle, but nothing was elicited, and when the raps on the table spelt out "done," we concluded that the spirits had departed, and we might as well leave also.

CHAPTER XV.

THE LYING SPIRIT.

We attended, one evening, a circle at a private dwell ing, where the following so called manifestations took place. When the circle had been formed around the table, we noticed among the company the same gentleman who related to us the story of his having seen the spirit of Oliver Blodge, the murderer. We have given the story, as told by this gentleman, in a former chapter of this work. The gentleman referred to, and who is also a medium, had no sooner settled himself in his seat, than he said:

"Is there any spirit here who wishes to communicate with me?"

"Yes."

"Will you touch me?"

"Yes."

"Then do it."

The medium immediately shrunk back for an instant, as if he had experienced some unpleasant sensation. He then stretched his hand to the company and said:

"I was touched here on my hand, and it felt very hot, as if a burning substance had been applied to it. See here."

And as the medium spoke, he pointed to a red spot of considerable size, which was plainly visible on the back of his hand.

The medium then addressing himself to the supposed spirit, continued his questions:

"What sphere are you in?"

"Third."

"Are you sure?"

"Yes."

"Will you spell out your name?"

"No."

(The above answers, together with all those recorded in this report, were given by tips of the table.)

After a few other questions, while the table or the supposed spirit did not answer with much willingness, the medium said to the supposed spirit:

"Can you read my mind?"

"Yes."

"Will you read it?"

"Yes."

The medium here paused a moment, as if he was submitting his thoughts to the examination of the supposed spirit. The medium then continued addressing the supposed spirit, as follows:

"Now you read my mind thoroughly, do you?"

"Yes."

"Then, by what you saw, in my mind, I charge you to speak the truth, and answer my questions. Will you answer truthfully?"

"Yes."

"Is it owing to the power of what you saw in my mind, that you will answer truthfully?"

"Yes."

"You dare not disobey me, dare you?"

"No."

"Was not your touch, on my had just now, hot?"

"Yes."

"Did you burn me?"

"Perhaps."

"You see this mark on my hand; did you make it?"

"Yes."

"Now what sphere are you in?"

"The first."

"Can I do anything for you to ameliorate your condition?"

The Medium asked this last question because the first sphere is supposed by spiritualists to be the lowest sphere, in fact, in which undeveloped spirits dwell.

"Can I do anything to ameliorate your condition?"

"Yes."

"What can I do for you; pray for you?"

"Yes."

"Will that help you?"

"Yes."

"Now spell out your name."

The Medium here took out the alphabet card, and the table tipped when he pointed to the letters, which, when put together, spelt the name of "Oliver Blodge."

"Did I not charge you," said the Medium, "never to come near me again."

"Yes."

"Why have you come then? Was you sent for?"

"Yes."

"For what—to make physical manifestations?"

"Yes."

"Did you ever appear before in any circle and say you were the spirit of Shakspeare?"

"Yes."

"Are you Shakspeare?"

"No."

"Do you wear a crown of gold on your head and dress in a purple robe?"

"No."

"Did you ever appear to Miss ——— wearing such a crown and dress?"

"No."

"How was it then—was it only a spectral illusion before her eyes?"

"Yes."

"Was that illusion formed by you for the purpose of deceiving Miss ———?"

"Yes."

"For what purpose—in order that your presence might be permitted?"

"Yes."

We have before described the appearance of Oliver Blodge, to the vision of Miss ———, in one of our former reports.

A thin, wiry person, whose expression of face was of that hard and impenetrable nature, which betokened that he was not likely to believe anything he could not see or feel, here remarked that he should be pleased to see the table tip from the medium.

In a moment the table was raised up instead of being depressed.

"Tip the table quickly," said the Medium.

The table was immediately raised by some unseen power, rapped down on the floor, and rocked to and fro with great velocity.

The thin, wiry man opened his eyes and gazed at the antics of the table with astonishment.

"Well," he at length said, when he had recovered his somewhat suspended breath, "this is most extraordinary. I've often tried to get such manifestations before. I have been to a great many circles, but I have always until now failed."

"It has doubtless been owing to the want of harmony in the circles which you visited that has caused your failure," remarked the Medium.

The thin wiry man now again said :—

"I should like to see the table rear up on the opposite side, where no person is seated."

After some apparent effort the table suddenly and with violence raised up on the side indicated by the thin wiry man, and in its raising up nearly knocked the thin wiry man over. The table then for a moment balanced itself on one leg, and then resumed its natural position.

The thin wiry man then asked some test questions, as they are called, such as his father's and his child's name, all of which were spelt out correctly, as he said, by the alphabet. The thin wiry man then left, and we soon followed him.

CHAPTER XVI.

THE SPIRIT OF FUDGE.

A FEW evenings after the manifestation of the "Lying Spirit," an account of which we have given in the preceding chapter, we were present at another private circle where the table was surrounded by some six or eight persons. There were several mediums present, all of whom were men.

The circle had no sooner been formed, than the tips of the table announced that some spirit was present, who wished to communicate with somebody.

"Who is the spirit?" said Medium No. 1. "Is it this?" and the Medium, as he spoke, wrote a name on a slip of paper.

There was no answer to this, except that Medium No. 1 had no sooner asked the question than he made in his throat a singular sort of a chuckle, as if he was endeavoring to suppress laughter. The company looked astonished, but the Medium continued to chuckle, and the company, who were mostly Spiritualists, came to the conclusion that the spirit which had manifested itself, whoever it was, was chuckling for some particular reason through the throat of the Medium, and that the Medium could not help chuckling.

"Well, chuckling spirit! since we cannot find out your name, please tell us what sphere you are in," said one of the company.

"First," answered Medium No. 1, whom it was supposed the chuckling spirit now possessed; and, when he had made this brief answer, he commenced to chuckle again.

Another Medium present, whom we shall designate as Medium No. 2, here gave evidence, by those violent spasms of the hand, which we have often described in these reports, that the spirit was about to move him to write. The spasmodic influence finally resulted in a dash at a piece of paper, and on the piece of paper Medium No. 2 wrote a name.

"Is that your name?" said he, holding up the paper and addressing himself to the chuckling spirit which was supposed to hold its influence over Medium No. 1.

The chuckle of Medium No. 1 broke short off, and from the mouth of the said Medium there came an emphatic "Yes." And the chuckle went on again.

The name which Medium No. 2 wrote on his paper, and which the chuckling spirit in Medium No. 1 answered was his name, was "Fudge."

A conversation now followed among the members of the circle as to the character and intentions of this chuckling spirit who called himself "Fudge." Some said that they thought they were being humbugged, and others remarked, with some slight manifestation of feeling, that they did not wish the spirit to make fun of them.

Medium No. 1 at this moment began to wring his hands, twist himself, and make sundry contortions of his face, as if he wished to relieve himself of the influence of the chuckling spirit called "Fudge."

"Spirit of Fudge! will you write, if you have anything to say to us?" said one of the circle, addressing Medium No. 1.

After some hesitation, Medium No. 1 wrote, with spasmodic effort, as follows:—

"As I know, that I can tell you, I can say only what I know. It is for you to digest that which is given to you. You are not so blind as to believe literally all the spirits say. If you do, you have yet to acquire your A, B, C. (Signed) FUDGE."

More conversation here ensued around the circle as to the nature of the spirit "Fudge," when suddenly Medium No. 1, through whom the alleged spirit was operating, became convulsed, and a loud Ha! ha! ha! burst from his lips.

"Well, Fudge, what do you mean by ha! ha! ha?" asked one of the circle.

"I am impressed," answered Medium No. 1, or rather "Fudge," in Medium No. 1, "to say that you are all fools."

"Is the impression of Medium No. 1 correct?" asked another of the circle, addressing himself to the table.

The table tipped once, meaning, thereby, "No."

Another ha! ha! ha! now rung from the lips of Medium No. 1, and soon afterwards he wrote spasmodically as follows :—

"You desired, if I impressed the Medium, when he said I had told him you were all fools. His impression was correct. I answered just now that it was not correct, because you desired it, and it would amuse you. You wish for a reason why I consider you fools : ask your own hearts. Do you come to learn, or from curiosity? If you come to learn, why is it that you seem but to indulge curiosity? Know you not that they who desire to learn do not dictate, but wait for the crumbs of knowledge, even as they fall, and receive them with thankfulness?

(Signed) FUDGE."

The supposed spirit of Fudge here paused a moment from his epistolary labor, as if to take rest; but soon after wrote again through the medium, as follows:

"When man desires to teach a child, does not the teacher lower his mind to the capacity of the child? Then shall it be wondered that the spirits should take the ingredient they find, and mould it by gradual shaping, until it is fitted to receive the impression intended to be conveyed? The mind to be teachable, must be even as the mind of a child. If in the strong exercise of its own will, how can it be accessible for impression? When will man learn that imperativeness is not the most teachable commodity. Ha! ha! ha!

(Signed) FUDGE."

The spirit of "Fudge" now departed. Medium No. 1 ceased to chuckle, and resumed his natural grave demeanor.

Another spirit was now called up by one of the circle, who asked if the spirit which he was addressing, was acquainted with the spirit of "Fudge," and to what sphere "Fudge" belonged?

The answer given by tips on the table, and by writing through one of the mediums, was in substance, that the spirit questioned, was not acquainted with the spirit of "Fudge," but had seen him; that "Fudge" did not belong to the first sphere, as he had stated, but that he belonged to a very high order of spirits; that the solution as to the answer which "Fudge" had made, that he was in the first sphere, was to be found in the peculiar phase of the minds of the members of the circle at that particular time, and that it was idle for any member of the circle to inquire for the sphere of the spirit as for authority; but the proper and true mode, was to judge a spirit by its communications; for untruthfulness is sometimes as characteristic of spirits as of mortals.

This was all that occurred at the circle where the spirit of "Fudge" manifested itself.

BOOK II.

THE RAPPERS

CONTEMPLATED PLEASANTLY, PHILOSOPHICALLY, AND THEOLOGICALLY.

CHAPTER I.

THE RAPPERS IN THE CONGRESS OF THE UNITED STATES.

WE stated in the commencement of our tour among the "Rappers," of the extent to which the doctrine of the "Rappers" had spread over the country, and the immense number of its proselytes. As illustrative of this, it will be appropriate here, at the commencement of our comments, for us to record, that the "Rappers have deemed themselves of sufficient importance to ask the attention of the Congress of the United States. On the 17th day of April, 1854, the "Rappers" rapped on the floor of Congress, in the following manner and to the following effect. On the day referred to, General Shields, United States Senator from Illinois, in Executive Session of the Senate, spoke as follows:

"I beg leave to present to the Senate a petition, with some fifteen thousand names appended to it, upon a very singular and novel subject. The petitioners represent that certain physical and mental phenomena of mysterious import, have become so prevalent in this country and Europe, as to engross a large share of public attention. A partial analysis of these phenomena, attest the existence, first, of an occult force, which is exhibited in sliding, raising, arresting, holding, suspending, and otherwise disturbing ponderable bodies, apparently in direct opposition to the acknowledged laws of matter, and transcending the accredited power of the human mind. Secondly, lights of different degrees of intensity appear in dark rooms, where chemical action or phosphorescent illumination cannot be developed, and where there are no means of generating electricity, or of producing combustion. Thirdly, a variety of sounds, frequent in occurrence, and diversified in character, and of singular significance and importance, consisting of mysterious rapping, indicating the presence of invisible intelligence. Sounds are often heard like those produced by the prosecution of mechanical operations, like the hoarse murmur of the winds and waves, mingled with the harsh creaking noise of the masts and rigging of a ship laboring in a sea. Concussions also occur, resembling distant thunder, producing oscillatory movements of surrounding objects, and a tremulous motion of the premises upon which these phenomena occur. Harmonious sounds, as those of human voices, and other sounds resembling those of the fife, drum, trumpet, &c., have been produced without any visible agency. Fourthly, all the functions of the human body and mind are influenced in what appear to be certain abnormal states of the system, by causes not yet adequately understood or accounted for. The occult force, or invisible power, frequently interrupts the normal operations of the faculties, suspending sensation and voluntary motion of the body to a death-like coldness and rigidity, and diseases hitherto considered incurable, have been entirely eradicated by this mysterious agency. The petitioners proceed to state that two opinions prevail with respect to the origin of these phenomena. One ascribes them to the power and intelligence of departed spirits operating upon the elements which pervade all natural forms. The other rejects this conclusion, and contends that all these results may be accounted for in a rational and satisfactory manner. The memorialists, while thus disagreeing as to the cause, concur in opinion as to the occurrence of the alleged phenomena; and in view of their origin, nature and bearing upon the interests of mankind, demand for them a patient, rigid, scientific investigation, and request the appointment of a scientific commission for that purpose. I have now given a faithful synopsis of this petition, which, however unprecedented in itself, has been prepared with singular ability, presenting the subject with great delicacy and moderation. I make it a rule to present any petition to the Senate, which is respectful in its terms; but having discharged this duty, I may be permited to say that the prevalence of this delusion at this age of the world, among any considerable portion of our citizens, must originate in my opinion, in a defective system of education, or in a partial derangement of the mental faculties, produced by a diseased condition of the physical organization. I cannot, therefore, believe that it prevails to the extent indicated in this petition. Different ages of the world have had their peculiar delusions. Alchemy occupied the attention of eminent men for several centuries; but there was something sublime in alchemy. The philosopher's stone, or the transmutation of base metals into gold—the *elixir vitæ* or "water of life," which would preserve youth and beauty, and prevent old age, decay, and death, were blessings which poor humanity ardently desired, and which alchemy sought to discover by perseverence and piety. Roger Bacon, one of the greatest alchemists and greatest men of the thirteenth century, while searching for the philosopher's stone, discovered the telescope, burning glasses, and gunpowder. The prosecution of that delusion led, therefore, to a number of useful discoveries. In the sixteenth century flourished Cornelius Agrippa, alchemist, astrologer, and magician, one of the greatest professors of hermetic philosophy that ever lived. He had all the spirits of the air and demons of the earth under his command. Paulus Jovious says that the devil in the shape of a large black dog, attended Agrippa wherever he went. Thomas Nash says, at the request of Lord Surrey, Erasmus, and other learned men, Agrippa called up from the grave several of the great philosophers of antiquity—among others, Sully, whom he caused to deliver his celebrated oration for Roscius, to please the Emperor, Charles IV. He summoned king David and king Solomon from the tomb, and the Emperor conversed with them long upon the science of government. This was a glorious exhibition of spiritual power, compared with the insignificant manifestations of the present day. I will pass over the celebrated Paracelsus, for the purpose of making allusion to an Englishman, with whose veracious history every one ought to make himself acquainted. In the sixteenth century, Dr. Dee made such progress in the talismanic mysteries, that he acquired ample power to hold familiar conversation with spirits and angels, and to learn from them all the secrets of the universe. On the occasion, the angel Uriel gave him a black crystal of a convex form, which he had only to gaze upon intently, and by a strange effort of the will, he could summon any spirit he wished, to reveal to him the secrets of futurity. Dee, in his veracious diary, says that one day while he was setting with Alburtus Laski, a Polish nobleman, there seemed to come out of the oratory a spiritual creature, like a pretty girl of seven or nine years of age, with her hair rolled up before and hanging down behind, with a gown of silk, of changeable red and green, and with a train. She seemed to play up and down, and to go in and out behind the books, and as she seemed to get between them, the books displaced themselves and made way for her. This I call a spiritual manifestation of the most interesting and fascinating kind. Even the books felt the fascinating influence of this spiritual creature; for they displaced themselves and made way for her. Edward Kelly, an Irishman, who was present, and who witnessed this beautiful apparition, verifies the docter's statement; therefore it would be unreasonable to doubt a story so well attested—particularly when the witness was an Irishman. Dr. D. was the distinguished favorite of kings and queens—a proof that spiritual science was in high repute in tho good old age of queen Elizabeth. But of all the professors of occult science, hermetic philosophy or spiritualism, the Rosicrucians were the most exalted and refined. With them the possession of the philosopher's stone was to be the means of health and happiness—an instrument by which man could command the services of superior beings, control the elements, defy the abstractions of time and space, and acquire the most intimate knowledge of all the secrets of the universe. These were objects worth struggling for. The refined Rosicrucians were utterly disgusted with the coarse, gross, sensual spirits who had been in communication with man previous to their day; so they decreed the annihilation of them all, and substituted in their stead, a race of mild, beautiful and beneficent beings. The spirits of the olden time were a malignant race, and took especial delight in doing mischief; but the new generation is mild and benignant. These spirits, as this petition attests, indulge in the most innocent amusements and harmless recreations—such as sliding, raising and tipping tables, producing pleasing sounds and variegated sights, and sometimes curing diseases which were previously considered incurable; and for the existence of this simple and benignant race our petitioners are indebted to the brethren of the rosy cross. Among the modern professors of spiritualism, Cagliostro was the most justly celebrated. In Paris his saloons were thronged with the rich and the noble. To old ladies he sold immortality, and to the young ones he sold beauty that would endure for centuries, and his charming countess gained immense wealth, by granting attendant sylphs to such ladies as were rich enough to pay for their services. The *Biographes des Contempores*, a work which our present mediums ought to consult with care, says there was hardly a fine lady in Paris who would not sup with the shade of Lucretius in the apartments of Cagliostro. There was not a military officer who would not discuss the art with Alexander, Hannibal or Cæsar, or an advocate or counsellor who would not argue legal points with the ghost of Cicero. These were spiritual manifestations worth paying for, and all our degenerate mediums would have to hide their demolished heads in the presence of Cagliostro. It would be a curious inquiry to follow this occult science through all its phases of mineral magnetism, animal mesmerism, &c., until we reach the present, latest and slowest phase of all spiritual manifestation; but I have said enough to show the truth of Burk's beautiful aphorism, "the credulity of dupes is as inexhaustible as the invention of knaves."

A pleasant debate followed after Senator Shields' speech. Mr. Petit proposed to refer the petition of the Spiritualists to three thousand clergymen. Mr. Weller proposed to refer it to the Committee on Foreign Relations, as it might be necessary to inquire whether or not when Americans leave this world they lose their citizenship. Mr. Mason proposed that it should be left to the Committee on Military Affairs. Gen. Shields himself said he had thought of proposing to refer the petition to the Committee on Post Offices and Post Roads, because there may be a possibility of establishing a spiritual telegraph between the material and spiritual worlds.

The petition was finally, by a decisive vote, laid upon the table. The table did not, as we learn, tip in indignation at this summary disposal of Spiritualism in the Senate, by which we must infer that the spirits, if there were any in the Senate at that time, endorsed its action and considered the same all right.

CHAPTER II.

PHILOSOPHICAL RAP PRELIMINARY.

In this chapter, we shall let an English author, J. G. Mac Walter, rap a few paragraphs for us, simply because they are appropriate, and form just the introduction which we wish. Mr. Mac Walter says:—

"The great celebrity of table-tapping, et cetera, if not surpassed, is equalled by the vast diversity of opinion which is abroad regarding it. The only unanimity it has provoked is—to disagree. No set of men, usually found to agree, hold similar views upon this subject, and each clings to an adopted notion with a pertinacity worthy of a better cause. Of course, there are exceptions to this rule. There are some who only ponder upon its general effects without either questioning its genuineness, or doubting its falsity; they are open to conviction, are impartial and deliberate. But there are others, who declare 'the whole thing incredible—a monstrous imposition.' Because they have never seen a table turn without physical action employed to produce motion, therefore no table has been turned after any other manner. They never heard a table-tapping—

never witnessed any of these alleged wonders—and therefore, with generous grace, they place all the alleged facts to the account of over-excited imagination—mere absurdities, neither Satanic nor natural. In fact, nothing but a huge and glaring mistake! Others, again, feel that as thousands of unimpeachable witnesses, with intellects every whit as keen as any skeptics, have testified to these marvels, they—even without actually having seen them themselves—ought not hastily to throw an atmosphere of doubt over each and all those cases which have been made public. It is not, indeed, easy to understand how great and penetrating men, like Judge Edmonds, could deliberately fabricate 'wonders,' or lend themselves to propagating as facts things of which they have even a shadow of doubt. Besides, if we reject the credibility of credible men, because their testimony *appears* strange, we do that for which, when pushed to its logical conclusion, we should be sorry; we practically cast from beneath us a grand and honored support. Many, doubtless, wishing, but unable to refuse this evidence, fancy that all these trustworthy witnesses have not sifted the matter sufficiently, or they might have detected, at least in the *table-tapping*, the effect of an ingenious mechanism—some toe-tapping, knee-rapping, bone-cracking, or crafty doings of the *media*, by means of some ingenious machinery. Others still consider the table-*turning* as the consequence of unconscious muscular action—so unconscious, indeed, that determined skeptics can hardly deny that it is truly strange, and nearly sufficient to work conviction. This, perhaps, is more plausible than satisfactory, and does not at all account for table-*tapping*.

"There are others, who, while they confess to a belief in extraordinary manifestations, hesitate to ascribe their origin to mechanical, natural, or supernatural agencies. They are fearful, sensitive, and over-credulous. Inclination induces them to lean towards the notion that mere mechanism is 'at the bottom of all;' but experience will not sanction what might appear an agreeable conclusion. These people are in a mist, which they reluctantly prefer to that unclouded light which a highly-wrought imagination renders them apprehensive of beholding.

"Another section boldly declare that all is plain enough to them in the matter,—as clear as 'noon-day,' —without explaining whether 'noon-day' be misty or not. They observe that strange—nay, astounding,— 'manifestations,' such as are beyond all reason, take place without the possibility of collusion, and they ask How can these be else than supernatural? But even more than that—they avow that it has been 'satisfactorily settled,' that all are evil *demon*strations—really Satanic; in fact, neither more nor less than a 'sign' that the end of the world is at hand, and that our great spiritual foe makes his presence manifest through the very tables on which we dine and sup, and which we turn to a variety of other pleasing purposes.

Some wiser people shake their heads significantly, and widely differ from the conclusions formed by all the others. They upbraid one party as hasty irrational, obdurate, and skeptical; they tell another that its theory of muscular pressure falls to the ground if a very weighty table moves—nay, lifts itself up, which is only *touched* by a feeble girl; and that such theory, moreover, cannot explain the rappings—the peculiar rappings—which accompany these movements. As for the tapping with the feet, and similar kinds of imposture, the nicest tests have put the possibility of such collusion out of the question, and left the mystery so far undisturbed. Respecting spirit interference, and all similar speculations, the singular evidences of deterioration in learning—in fact, the inexcusable ignorance—which the supposed spirits exhibit, are justly held up as a practical refutation of any such notion.

It is, in truth, singular that men who were *here* of high attainments, turn out at the rapping *séances* to be hardly able to spell even their own names correctly. Besides, the presumed presence of spirits is quite incompatible with all revealed knowledge. Those who thus rationally think, hold, in opposition to all other theorists, that the several conditions upon which the so-called manifestations depend, are human and earthly, and can in no wise be attributed to disembodied spirits; that, though the effects appear so startling, they can be traced to known natural laws, and are the effects of a simple cause.

CHAPTER III.

A SERIES OF PHILOSOPHICAL RAPS ON THE RAPPERS, OR A DIGEST OF OPINIONS, PRO AND CON.

"Alas!" exclaims the American, Hawthorne, in his "Blithedale Romance," when touching incidentally on the subject: "Alas! methinks we have fallen on an evil age! If these phenomena have not humbug at the bottom, so much the worse for us. What can they indicate in a spiritual way, except that the soul of man is descending to a lower point than it has ever reached while incarnate? We are pursuing a downward course in the eternal march, and thus bring ourselves into the same range with beings whom death—in requital of their gross and evil lives—has degraded below humanity. To hold intercourse with spirits of this order, we must stoop and grovel in some element more vile than earthly dust. These goblins, if they exist at all, are but the shadows of past mortality—mere refuse stuff, adjudged unworthy of the eternal world, and as the most favorable supposition, dwindling gradually into nothingness. The less we have to say to them, the better, lest we share their fate."

An American medium, Mr. Cooley, of Springfield, admits that these phenomena are of human origin; that they are the result of electric or magnetic conditions, and that there is every possibility of reducing them to demonstration, and as this mode of solution is gradually obtaining ground, it is probable that the tone of the "Rappists" will gradually lower in proportion as they find themselves unsupported. Man, however, is an impartial creature, and especially when his curiosity is excited. What he cannot decide upon for himself, he feels thankful if any other will do so for him.

A Rev. Mr. Godfrey propounds a theory of satanic agency, energizing itself in the inert legs of tables, and finds the spirits of the swine synonymous with epilepsy and madness. "The table," says Mr. Godfrey, "was more sagacious than a dog, and more obedient than a child. My impression is, that the placing the hands on the table, is a sort of incantation. By it the sitters signify their wish to be brought into communication with the spirit-world. They sit until they are observed by some one of the wandering spirits, who thereupon enters the table, making it crack at the moment of its entering in. The reason why it will not obey any commands, *unless hands are placed on*, has suggested an idea, which, if it be true, is a very solemn one. It occurred to me, while writing, that the table '*moved simply by the laying on of hands.*' 'This moral nothing,' (the table,) '*on the imposition of your hands, begins to live!*' Can it be that this is the beginning of Satan's last struggle—that *on the imposition of hands*, the table is endued with power from the devil, as the Lord's servants, *on the imposition of hands*, were, in the apostle's days, endued with power *from on high?* I merely ask, can it be?"

An European Journal, called the ZOIST, a tolerably well-known, and, in some respects, a well-edited journal, strenuously advocating the doctrines of Mesmer, waits upon a medium, and gives us, with a certain significance of meaning, the preliminaries this wise: "The spirits are at times dilatory in making their presence known, which the medium accounts for in some such way as the prophet of old sarcastically hinted at the absence of Baal, but sooner or later they arrive, sometimes not till half an-hour has elapsed, and then expectation is the more highly worked up, and *so much the less time is left for rigorous examination.* There is heard a faint rap at the table: so faint perhaps that the medium says, 'Hush—stop: I heard a rap.' All listen; it is repeated; one hears it, and then another also hears it, and so on, till all agree that the rapping has begun, and the spirits have certainly arrived. All are now amazed, and all are attentive. The gentlemen become grave; the ladies pale; and all are satisfied that there is something in it. The sound is like the pecking of a bird; like a slight striking of the edge of a finger-nail upon a hard substance; and sometimes the sound is of a stronger hitting; all may be well imitated by striking the edge of a finger-nail upon a table with various degrees of force. The idea of anything peculiar, awful, unearthly in the sound, is ridiculous. There are slight raps from little children, strong ones from gentlemen spirits, and soft raps from lady spirits."

The result was a tissue of hazarded solutions to questions put, in which bad grammar and vile spelling were only surpassed by the ludicrous extent of the mistakes. A gentleman at the conclusion took a letter from his pocket, and the spirit present was asked if it would be so kind as to tell the name of the writer. It at once knocked assent, but made a most unlucky miss: neither surname nor Christian name was rapped right; and words were rapped out as different from the true as Jeremy Diddler is from Isaac Newton. And, why? "*Because he held the alphabet under the table, so that the medium could not see it in his hand*, and he kept his eyes fixed on one spot." Now however ungallant such a proceeding might have been, it is quite evident that the "dominant impression" of the visitor is caught by the acute medium, who, with a certain force of character, must read the questioner, and if he or she cannot anticipate the question, every care is taken to *direct* the question, and to have it put, varied, shifted, and repeated in such form that the general correctness of any replies is thus by no means difficult to be accounted for.

"Household Words," by Charles Dickens, has not been much more favorable to the pretensions of the "spiritual manifestations." The grave irony of this admirable periodical is deepened into a fierce and sarcastic bitterness in Blackwood, who, laughing at the whole theory, practice, professors, and visitors, as dupers and dupes, pours the whole phial of his ungovernable wrath on their devoted heads.

In "Chambers' Journal," we find that the examination has been conducted with considerable care; and an evident desire to be assured of the conscientious truth prevents the writer from coming to an actual decision,—whereby spirits and "mediums" receive the benefit of all doubts that may exist in their favor.

An M. A. writing from Cambridge, describes, at some length, the results of an interview with a medium, Mrs. H., and bears testimony to the fact, that, in the majority of instances, the questions (of an intricate kind, too) which he propounded were satisfactorily answered; and while something like a suspicion came over him, that while the replies were being given, the solution of the mystery was to be found in the circumstance of his pausing on such correct letters as a quick-sighted and practised medium might easily notice. This was negatived, however, by the fact that replies were also correct when the card was hidden. Even questions asked mentally, by himself and others present, and whose veracity he could trust in, terminated in the same satisfactory manner.

"At a third interview," continues our Cambridge M. A., "my time for questioning was very limited, but the following curious circumstance occurred:—I resolved to have some communication with which my own mind could have nothing to do in the way of influence. I received the following, which I give exactly as it was rapped out, that is, without any distinction of words or sentences [a necessary feature in all these communications, as the reader will at once perceive.] 'What say estth ouaproof b roth ergodwill give you?' The sense was not clear (indeed I thought it was all nonsense that I was getting)—until the end of the communication, when it appeared that the communication was: 'What sayest thou?—a proof, brother, God will give you! The word 'brother' struck me as merely a common *formula;* and, not having the most distant idea to whom I was indebted for this communication, I asked if the 'invisible' would favor me with his name. The answer was 'James." Now as I did not, at the moment, recollect any friend of mine in the spirit-world of that Christian name, I immediately thought of an old college friend of mine, who, however, is still living. So I next asked if it was any relation? 'Yes.' What relation? 'Brother.' And it was not till this moment that it occurred to me that I had a brother of that name who died when I was only a few months old, of whom, therefore, as the reader may suppose, I am not much in the habit of thinking."

Strange as all this is, it is not so entirely inexplicable but that the spirits may be wholly dispensed with. In the scheme of Mesmerism, it is admitted that there is such a thing as *thought-reading*, besides the striking phenomena of clairvoyance; so that while the mesmerized patient can pierce walls and space, and give a catalogue of the furniture of a strange house, or describe correctly persons who—there may be reason to suppose—have not before been known to the patient, he (or she, for the female is more susceptible to the magnetic current than the male) can read the thought and reply to the unspoken question that is passing in the mind.

The pulpit has not been slow, in eminent instances, to accept the spiritual explanation, but insists that the spirits are evil, and that the whole is of satanic origin. Some time back, the Rev. Dr. Tyng, an Episcopal clergyman, and rector of St. George's church, New-York, in a sermon, warned his hearers against having aught to say or do with these spirits. Without denying or appearing to doubt the whole allegement of facts, he seems to have taken them for granted. Nor is that difficult if the power of the "prince of the air" is admitted to possess equal extent and energy as formerly.

From the "Paris Journal of Magnetism," a periodical of considerable pretensions, we feel tempted to take an extract, which still more reduces to the magnetic influence the bold claims of these manifestations to spiritual; and with such consistence as can be expected from a work ostensibly devoted to the propagation of the magnetic theory, clearly points out where the solution is, sooner or later, to be found by those who feel an interest in seeking it.

The letter appears under the signature of "Anna Blackwell,"—"I have myself been present on one occasion only with a lady, a friend of mine, a distinguished writer, whom you well know yourself, at a private meeting, at Mr. Stone's house. We waited upwards of two hours before the rapping could or would be heard, except in slight and distant taps. A second medium, a young girl belonging to London, in whom the faculty has recently declared itself spontaneously, and who was present, told us that we must be patient; for they would soon have prepared 'the battery,' and that already a crowd of our friends were there, and ready to communicate with us as soon as the telegraph should be in a state to act. During this long suspense, the table frequently became as if charged with electricity, and we felt, instead of shocks, a series of continual vibrations, as well as in the floor, the chairs, &c. Another table, standing between ours and the windows, was likewise made to vibrate, and distant taps becoming audible from it, we seated ourselves round it to try whether it might not succeed better than our own. Shortly after the taps ordered the young girl to go, with the rest of the operators, into another room, saying that her fluid thwarted that of Mrs. Haydon, the medium of Mr. Stone, and that they would talk with us as soon as we should be left alone with them. This was done, and strange noises, which we heard for the first time, filled the apartment, sounding all at the same time, so that it was not easy to distinguish one of them from another. But having contrived to learn the taps from some friends who declared themselves to be there—an easy matter, since each tap has its own note as distinguishable as the voice—I held with several of these strange communicators entire conversations, some of them absolutely intellectual, which fully convinced me that I was occupied with a being perfectly acquainted with my former career, and thoroughly sure of what he was saying. In reply to my mental questions, they quoted proper names, dates, &c.—spelled by means of the alphabet with perfect accuracy. As my friend herself was ignorant of the greater part of the facts alluded to by the taps, and as Mrs. Haydon, whom we both saw for the first time, knew no more than herself, it is evident that the medium, unless endowed with the faculty of clairvoyance to an almost miraculous degree—and it appears she did not possess it at all—could take no part in these answers.

"Frankly speaking, Mr. Editor, you yourself, who have long known me as a rational person, can you believe that on that evening I felt, or thought I felt, a hand upon my left heel? The pressure of the thumb on one side, and of the fingers on the other, was so well copied, that I at first imagined that somebody had stolen beneath my chair, and yet there was no one there; and it would have been impossible for either of these two ladies to touch me in that manner, without stooping, even had not their hands been at the time on the table.

"Since then another lady of my acquaintance, whilst she was trying to hold a table which would not be still, and on which she had laid her hands, had that hand severely pinched, and a ring which she wore was pulled with so much violence as to be broken in two. These pieces were drawn out in length another shape, so much altered, that it was impossible to join them."

CHAPTER IV.

DIGEST OF OPINIONS CONTINUED—A SCIENTIFIC SOLUTION.

It is well that we can direct attention to arguments far more stable and tangible than any we have as yet had to deal with. Mr. E. C. Rogers, an American writer, has a very able and elaborate explanation of the spiritual rapping phenomena, which we shall now briefly notice.

Mr. Rogers credits the existence of a newly discovered *physical* agent, "distinct from electricity, but closely allied with animal magnetism," and which is identical with the od or odylic force of Baron Reichenbach. This force can be traced in two distinct forms of operation; one is totally independent of a presiding intelligence—the other exhibits the phenomena of intelligence ruling and guiding it. It thus becomes prevision—intelligent clairvoyance—acts at a distance *through* matter and space, and thus produces all the phenomena that have been attributed to direct spiritual agency.

We are led on by a series of the nicest deductions, through a whole mass of attested physical phenomena, in which electricity can be clearly discovered as primary causation, until we arrive at that point where the line divides the invisible and the impalpable from the material and the actual—that transition boundary, where spirit and body blend; where the one becomes in a manner the other, and the positive characteristics of both are undistinguishable and undefinable by any technology yet invented. If we remember that the mysteries of alchemy have been transferred to the precise laws of chemistry, and that the fearful wonders of astrology have assumed the sublime principles of astronomy, we shall not be much mistaken if, sooner or later, the mysteries of electro biology and odylic phenomena be not reducible to as exact proportion, and become subject to laws as well defined, as any that are recognizable in the arena of the material world at the present hour. Science and discovery have done so much to render the (alleged) impossible possible, that we neither doubt nor despair. Let us notice, then, the tendency of Mr. Rogers' doctrines.

The somnambulic trances, and odyle-magnetic condition of Angélique Cottin, and of Frederica Hauffe, in addition to others of less magnitude, but equal importance, are taken as the text of certain corollaries to be deduced therefrom, which amount to the following. The fact itself is very evident, that physical agents—subtle, unseen—are everywhere at work. "Force shows itself," as Somerville remarks, "in everything that exists in the heavens or on the earth. It pervades every atom—rules the motions of animate and inanimate beings; and is as sensible in the descent of a rain-drop, as in the falls of Niagara—in the weight of the air as in the periods of the moon." There is a physical power which "not only binds satellites to their planet, and planets with suns, and sun with sun, throughout the wide extent of creation, which is the cause of the disturbances as well as of the order of nature," but it physically binds man to man, and man to nature. And, as "every tremor it excites in one planet is immediately transmitted to the furtherest limits of the system, in oscillations, which correspond in their periods with the cause producing them, like sympathetic notes in music, or vibrations from the deep tones of an organ," so every vibration thus excited, is transmissible to the delicate centres of every organic being, provided the repulsive agent of those beings is changed in its relative condition, so as to admit the influx.

That the characteristics of this "force" differ from those of electricity, as commonly educed, appears from the circumstances attending the touching of Angélique Cottin, when a person would receive what really seemed a true electric shock, yet Arago could not detect the characteristics of electric agency. He noticed that the north pole of the magnet gave Angélique Cottin a powerful shock, and the south pole produced no effect upon her; but he could not detect the least influence from her organism upon the magnetic needle; and yet a powerful force from her body would overturn tables, and raise a heavy weight without contact. Not only so, but at times these outward things would attract her towards them—"Thus," argues a sound professor of science, "demonstrating the action and *re*action of the same agent, and that, whatever the force was, it *acted* *from the tables* and *other objects upon her*—that therefore it resided with *them* as well as with her—that consequently, it was a common inorganic, physical agent, susceptible, under favorable circumstances, of a most powerful action from the laboratory of the animal organs. Moreover, the facts throughout show that the condition required for this unusual evolution of force, is a specific variation of the organism from its normal condition. It is evident, therefore, that this agent is *not the vital organic agent, nor a part of it,* though the former is associated with the latter in the organism. We are not to conclude, however, that this is the only inorganic agent which is associated with the vital force. It is well known that electricity has its place among the other forces in the animal economy—so has heat—but they are "principles found universally in nature."

"Vitality," says Dr. Wm. F. Channing, "is dependent on physical conditions, and performs its functions by the agency of physical forces. A distinction thus exists between the principle itself and the agents by which its results in the living structure are accomplished. This distinction is an essential one, and constitutes the basis of any system which proposes to act directly on the vital forces. The *agents employed by the animal organization, are principles found* UNIVERSALLY IN NATURE; and, in addition to these, a force which is peculiar to living structures, the special agent of vitality." Now, it might reasonably be expected, that if electricity, among other agents found "universally in nature," is also associated with the agent of the animal economy, it might, under favorable conditions, exhibit its characteristic phenomena.

It is well known to every chemist, that wherever there is chemical action, there is an evolution of electricity. Now the vital force is constantly keeping up a chemical action in the animal organism ; it must therefore follow that there is a constant evolution of electric agency in that organism. The experiments of Matteucci upon the muscles of animals, show that they act as elements of a voltaic pile. Thus, when we connect the interior and the surface of the muscles of a living or recently killed animal by means of a conducting arc, the existence of an electric current is then vigorously demonstrated. The current is always directed from the interior to the exterior of the same muscles. It exists without the direct influence of the nervous system, and is not modified even when we destroy the integrity of the latter. It is not, however, from the nutrition of the muscular system alone that the evolution of electricity takes place; nor is it to chemical action alone that it can be attributed. It is well known to philosophers that every change of matter, however slight, occasions an electric development. There is not a muscular movement, voluntary or involuntary, that does not break up portions of the organism into particles. Neither is there a motion of the brain, indeed, by thought, passion, or emotion, that does not produce the same effect. This change of matter in the organism—this constant disintegration, must therefore constantly evolve the electric agency. Respiration, circulation, digestion, secretion, and so forth, are constantly giving freedom to this force. These opinions, the many experiments of Thilorier, Lafontaine, and others, confirmed in a lengthy paper laid before the Academy of Paris. These are essentially affirmative of Reichenbach's odic force, the more enlarged features of which are its independence of the usual conductors, or rather its capacity for transforming negative into positive conductors, and the like. Reichenbach found this force as it emanated from the organism, transmissible "not only through metals, but also glass, rosin, silk, &c., as if they were perfect conductors." The analogy here is beyond all question on this ground. MM. Thilorier and Lafontaine, with their new agent, Matteucci, with his anomalous agent, and Reichenbach, with his odyle, met in common. When the free odic force is thus accumulated in a body, it is retained in it in such a manner that it does not readily escape, as is the case with electricity. This is what takes place in the case of some mediums, who become powerfully charged with the odic force; and it is under the circumstances of a sudden change of the nerve-centres of the organism that this force escapes, as was witnessed in the case of Angélique Cottin. At one moment, there were in her case, severe nervous paroxysms, a tremor of the muscles, and at one instant everything would be overthrown which she touched, or even approached without touching. Now, the difference between the case of Angélique Cottin and that of the so-called "mediums" of the present day, with regard to the discharge of the odic force, is this:—With the former, the cause of the discharge lay wholly in the sympathetic and spinal nerve-centres. The unusual accumulation of this force, in the first place, was caused by a peculiar abnormal action of the lower sympathetic nerves, mostly connected with the uterine functions. This accumulation of force arrived at its maximum between the hours of seven and nine in the evening. Its infringement upon the spinal system at the time of its discharge, caused the spasms. The muscles also became charged with it from the sympathetic centres, causing their tremor ; and, what is worthy of observation, the parts where the discharge of this force was very intense, would have a peculiar trembling, " which," says Arago, "communicated itself to the head which touched the parts." We say that the difference between this case and the " mediums of the present day, in whose presence tables are moved, sometimes without touching, is that the force in the case of Angélique, discharged itself by causes acting below the psychological centres; whereas the discharge of the force from the organism of the " mediums," is more at the command of the brain centres.

It is clearly established, at all events, that the magnet which has been developed in the experiments of mesmerizers is not an exclusive agent of the human organism, but is a universal force in nature. That, inasmuch as the human nerves, and the centres of the brain, are peculiarly susceptible to its influence, the whole outward material world is, through the medium of this agent, brought into an intimate relation to the centres of the human organism. Furthermore, as one human brain stands in a closer relation to another human brain than it does to a mere inorganic point, it follows, that it should be more susceptible to its influence; and since this influence takes place without necessarily involving the action of the mind, that it is *not* therefore necessarily connected with the spiritual world.

The subject debated by Rogers, regarding the force which was developed *without* an intelligent direction, soon opens out into proportions far more important, and introduces us to a force, the same in essence, that *has* an intelligent direction.

The grand question now, and that which the community most anxiously wait upon for a satisfactory answer is, Whence this intelligence? How is the table, the chair, made to move as by a law of intelligence? And how is it that the medium's hand is made to move, without his own free-will, with tenfold the rapidity in intelligent words than the medium can voluntarily execute? In short, Whence is all this apparent intelligence, without the conscious effort of any mortal present?

Carrying the argument still farther, to the theory of impressions as giving dominancy to the mind in an automatic and pre-sensatorial state, we think that the idea can be very plainly stated thus:

That an impression may be made upon the brain, or any part of it, in accordance with the law of sympathy, and then outwardly reflected in involuntary action, has been often demonstrated. Iodine and bromine on the daguerreotype plate, through the medium of light, receive an impression of objects brought within the focus of the camera. This may be said to be by a chemical law. True, and so when an image is impressed upon the retina of the eye through the same medium. It is not only, however, through the medium of light that impressions are made, but also through the medium of every form of imponderable or primary agency—through heat, magnetism, electricity, and odyle.

In this process the same thing takes place that transpires every day ; so that it is not necessary that a person should be thrown into a mesmeric trance in order that an impression may be made, or a predilection of the brain effected. It is strange that it has not been seen that the mesmeric phenomena are but the *extreme* developments of the common principles of humanity—*the law*, says Rogers, *of every man's every day life.* It is the property of the brain to receive impressions, but it is the prerogative of the self-conscious, self-determining, disciplined mind to reject or to receive their influence. And this is the reason why a highly-disciplined mind prevents a person from becoming a medium. An undisciplined mind has not a control over the brain, therefore it cannot prevent the influence of others in making impressions upon it; and, when made, it cannot prevent their reflex action, or reflection back upon the outward world. This is also why, in order to develope a medium, a suspended state of the mind, a passive will, is found necessary. This condition is precisely the same with that which the mesmerist requires.

The pre-established conditions are, therefore, first, a

non-controlling state of the mind as to the action of the brain under the influence of external agencies; second, a consequent readiness, on the part of the brain, to be played upon by the external agencies; and, third, a promptness of the brain to give a reflex action of these impressions back upon the outward world, through the medium of the automatic apparatus, in the bodily frame, or through the odylic force, that, it is clear, emanates from it. Coming now to the "intelligent power," it follows that the material agent that produces the raps is controllable by the peculiar changes that take place in the organs of the brain. To have this fairly understood, a fact, familiar to all scientific persons, may be stated. It is this: whenever a change of matter takes place, the primary physical agent that especially belongs to that form of matter is evolved. For illustration: if you take a strip of sheet iron, about three-fourths of an inch wide, by four or five inches long, and hold it in the magnetic dip of the earth, so that the lower end shall reach within an inch of the north-pole of a magnetic needle, and, in this condition, give it a sudden twist (one hand being at each end of the iron) the needle will act as if struck with a stick, when indeed no visible thing has touched it. In such experiments over a delicate needle, Rogers, by varied twistings of the iron under varying circumstances, produced nearly a hundred varying results upon the needle.

It is, no doubt, the prerogative of every man's mind or spirit to control the motions, and consequently the changes of his brain within prescribed limits; but, when the condition of the latter is such as a mesmeric trance and the like, the man's own personality is suspended in its prerogative action. The predominant influence upon it then becomes material—sensuous. Then the reflex action of another's brain will readily take place. Another's wish or request will act as law. But if we assume the agent engaged in the physical phenomena to be a spiritual agent, independent of the medium, then, allowing the will of the medium to control it, we have a human will controlling an independent spirit's will. This absurd and quite untenable notion is very dogmatically held by many spirit-rappers, who contend that the table, or whatever it may be, "moans and speaks" under the compelled influence of disembodied spirits!

Speaking of a fictitious identity induced into the brain, which loses all apprehension of self, and becomes individualized with that of another, by which there arises synchronism of thought and idea in a sort of prophetic transport, Mr. Rogers says, that, in some instances, a diseased action induced upon the organ adapted to the mind's sense of personality, will, in forms of this derangement, represent itself as God, in another will represent the personality of our Saviour, in another that of a mouse, and so on to a toad, a shilling bit, a stone, a—nothing, according to the accompanying conditions. The same thing takes place in sleep, trance, somnambulism, and clairvoyance. Professor Gregory, in speaking on such a subject, mentions several illustrative cases. Among them was that of a clairvoyant, who in this state described a locality in Caffraria. While describing himself as flying through the air, he all at once began "to appear uneasy and alarmed, and told me," says the Professor, "that he had fallen into the water, and would be drowned if I did not help him. I commanded him to get out of the water, and, after much actual exertion and alarm, he said he had got to the brink. He then said that he had fallen into a river in Caffraria, at a place where a friend of his was born. What seemed very remarkable was, that he spoke of the river, the field, farm-houses, people, animals, and woods, as if perfectly familiar to him; and told me he had spent many years in that country, whereas he has never been out of Scotland." Now, no one will contend that this state of the young man belonged to the personal, conscious self, the identical *me* of the man. The action of that rod yielded to the suspension of the normal consciousness, the reason, and the will. The remaining action, therefore, was that of the brain centred under the influence of impressions.

Mr. Rogers has known persons, on first becoming subjects of the "intelligent" phenomena of the "raps," to exercise a conscious control, as to the character or manner of phenomenal developments, but, on becoming more deeply inducted, the brain became subject, in specific ways, to external influences, entirely independent of the "desire, or "wish," or "will" of the medium. Then, all seemed so foreign from the real personality of the individual, as to induce him to believe himself subject to the influence of heavenly visitants. The same thing has been observed by Mr. Ballou. "It is a remarkable fact," says he, "that some mediums, who, during the first few days or weeks of their mediumship, knew themselves to have considerable power over the manifestations, have gradually become clear and passive, and found themselves, at last, utterly unable to affect the responses and communications made through them. For several weeks after he found himself a medium, he could get very much such answers to questions as he pleased. During that stage of his mediumship he felt quite confident the whole thing was but a new species of "mesmerism." But after a while he began to fail of controlling the agency, and at length found it operating entirely independent of his most determined "wishings and willings." The power is allowed within the influence of the "wishing" and the "willing" energy. The "wishing" and the "willing" are within the consciousness. But it is the "wishing" and the "willing" that in any case produce the phenomena directly. The "wishing" and the "willing" cannot take place in the brain, without at the same instant effecting a change of the matter of the brain. And it is by a change of matter that odylic agent (as in the case with electricity) is affected—eliminated. Now, whether this change of matter takes place in consequence of an action of the "will," or a "wish," or a conscious emotion, nothing but one of these three will be known to the mind, whereas the change of matter will be unconscious, and the consequent emanation of the physical agent will, therefore, be unconsciously affected, unless it interfere with the sensorium. But avoiding this, there will be no conscious knowledge of the physical emanation.

This fact is clearly exhibited where the medium's characteristic, bad orthography, is distinguished in the "raps." There is, however, no wish, no desire, no will, for such a result. There the habit of action lies in the brain—the tendency of the organ of language to act in a particular manner when excited is also there. We find, then, that certain words are always unconsciously spelled wrongly, whether the medium writes or spells the words vocally in the usual state, or whether she is acting in her professional capacity. In this latter case, she does not think of the words that are to be rapped out, nor of the letters that are to be thrown together to compose these words, and yet *her* orthography comes out true to the habit of her orthographic organ; otherwise, why should the "raps" come on precisely those letters she would herself use in a word if writing to a friend?

In the face of such scientific evidence alone, we reckon that the assumption of a supernatural agency is as absurd as it is dangerous. It is worse than precipitate to attribute to the influence of disembodied spirits, that which so evidently lies within the sphere of the human organization, human relations, and mundane agencies. Applying the arguments thus based, and any reasonable inference deducible therefrom, Mr. Rogers has given us an analysis as subtle, as we must say, it appears to be most severely tested by the laws of logic—to the principles which produced that dominancy—the phenomena of the divining rod · as also to the magnetic trances, not only of the Delphic Pythoness, but of the Seeress of Prevorst. It is inferred that all those cases where the phenomenon of movement of the divining rod takes place, the movement depends upon a specific relation of the nervous system to the emanation of this mundane agent, as the emanation of od from metallic substances and subterranean currents of water. It follows, therefore, that it is the same mundane agent that Reichenbach has discovered and named Od. But here it must be observed, that it is not the external od alone,—it is that in conjunction with the od of the human organism. It is the latter, then, that gives the characteristic phenomenon of the movement of the stick; and it is because the od force from the particular locality is specifically related to the od force of the organism, and the action of the one in relation to the action of the other, that the stick moves. In haunted houses the like conditions are fulfilled—namely, the emanations of mundane force in relation to specific conditions of human organisms, especially the nerve-centres. Where these conditions are permanently established, a dwelling will be permanently "haunted." And not only dwellings, but particular localities, in hilly and mountainous regions especially, will be haunted spots. In such a place a man will not only hear strange sounds, but he will (as Goethe and the Seeress of Prevorst at one time,) see his own ghost. For it is in this mundane imponderable that the organic form of animal and man can reflect itself with all its characteristics. It is on this that every human being impresses the peculiarities of his life in the world; so that, after the material form itself has gone to decay, its representation—its ghost—still exists, as that of the star, Alpha Lyra, which would still play its influence twenty years after the star itself had been blotted out of existence. When the nervous organization of an individual is brought into *rapport* with this mundane imponderable, the action of the former will have its exact counterpart repeated in another place, even at a distance. Strange as this may seem to those who have never thought upon the thousands of phenomena attesting it, it is nevertheless a fact of nature.

CHAPTER V.

ANOTHER SCIENTIFIC SOLUTION.

ANOTHER American author, Mr. J. B. Dods, explains the modern spirit manifestations as they are called, such as rapping, writing, moving furniture, &c., on the principles of what he calls the voluntary and involuntary powers of the mind. He says that these manifestations are produced by allowing the involuntary powers of the mind in the back brain to take the place and execute the office of the voluntary powers of the mind in the front brain, and through the muscular and nervous force to give motion to the medium's foot or any part of the body, over which the medium, at that instant, has no more control than any other person who may be in the room with him. "The manifestations," says Mr. Dods, "are occasioned by too great a redundancy of electricity, congregated upon the involuntary nerves, through the passivity of the mind, and thus imparting to them extraordinary nervous force. And this force will be, more or less, in the same ratio that they are thrown out of balance with the voluntary nerves. In this condition, an electro-magnetic discharge from the fingers or toes of the medium may often produce an audible snap, or even sound, by coming in contact with surrounding substances favorable to the propagation of sound, and be heard at considerable distances. And, moreover, the sound will appear to originate in the very spot where it is heard. Or this electro-magnetic force, by endeavoring to equalize itself throughout the nervous system of the medium, may occasion a snapping in the head, or a striking together of the joints, that can be heard in an adjoining room, and even appear to be in the room. And while these phenomena are transpiring, that part of the body in which they occur will be entirely destitute of feeling at the very instant that each sound or rap is given. *The entire passivity of the voluntary powers of the mind and of the voluntary nerves is the cause of unduly charging the involuntary powers with too great an electro-nervous force, and the result is those singular manifestations that are so confidently attributed to the agency of spirits.* After being thus charged, the voluntary powers have, doubtless, some agency in producing the sounds by a concentrated expectation, thus aiding the involuntary powers to produce an equilibrium, for there is a sympathetic connection between the two forces.

Hence persons who are in a perfectly cataleptic state, and which is, at the same time, attended with a brilliant clairvoyance, are sometimes capable of producing electro-magnetic sounds from their own involuntary nervous force, so as to be heard at a considerable distance. And being so near a state approaching the dead, and so sympathetically affected *en rapport* with the dying, that they often receive an impression, not only of the time the person dies, but also that the departed spirit, on its journey to future scenes, appears to, and addresses them."

Mr. Dods thus explains his theory of the *voluntary* and *involuntary* powers of the mind:

"We move the head, the eyes, the tongue, and lips, by the voluntary powers of the mind, and by the same power we move a finger, or the hands and arms to handle, and the feet and limbs to walk. At will we bend the body and ply every joint of the entire system. This, all are aware, is effected by the *voluntary powers* of the mind residing in the front brain, acting through the voluntary nerves. But over the motions of the heart, lungs, the circulation of the blood, the digestion of the food by the stomach, and all those movements on which the functions of life depend—over these we have no voluntary control. Awake or asleep, the heart continues to beat whether we will or not, and all the phenomena of life proceed as usual in their destined course. All these movements are produced by the *involuntary powers* of the mind residing in the back brain, acting through the involuntary nerves, and are not the result, as has been uniformly supposed, of mere organic life entirely distinct from mind. That these two forces both belong to mind is certain, because take the spirit from the body, and all motion, both voluntary and involuntary, instantly ceases. Hence, all the energies of reason, thought, understanding, consciousness, and will, belong exclusively to the voluntary powers of the mind. And all the movements on which the functions of life depend, and all the instinctive energies or intuitions of our being, belong to the involuntary powers of the mind. Hence, man has his instincts superior to all creatures in existence, and mind, like every other faculty in man, is double.

"We perceive, then, that the voluntary power of the mind can move or suspend motion, can act or cease acting, can reason, think, understand, and will, or suspend all these, as in sleep. But the involuntary power of the mind continues its ceaseless self-motion through every period of existence, when we are asleep as well as when awake. It has no power to stop, because motion is an inherent attribute of its nature. Seeing, hearing, feeling, taste, and smell, belong to the involuntary powers of the mind, where all impressions through the senses are first received, and from thence are instantly transmitted to the voluntary powers of the mind, where they are compared and formed into ideas by the power of what we term reason and association. Though the voluntary and involuntary powers of the mind are entirely distinct attributes, belonging to two distinct brains, yet there is, at the same time, an indissoluble connection existing between the two, and also a strong sympathy to concur together in one common state and mode of action, through indulgence and habit."

Mr. Dods cites a great many striking illustrations from ancient and modern history to prove his theory, that all the spirit manifestations which have transpired among mediums, such as involuntary writing, involuntary mesmerizing, involuntary speaking, involuntary table-tipping, involuntary rapping, arise from the mysterious movements and operations of the involuntary powers of the human mind, acting through the involuntary nerves. He accounts for the intelligence connected with these involuntary motions in the following manner:

"Every part of the human system, we may say, is double. We have two hands, two feet, two glands of taste, two eyes, and two ears. The heart is double, having its two auricles and two ventricles, and so is even the circulating system double—the *arterial* and *venous*. The human brain is likewise double, and so is the mind, that pervades and actuates it, also double. The *positive* and *negative* forces respond to, and balance each other, and pervade all nature. We have, in reality, two distinct brains, each performing its own distinct office, so long as they are kept in proper harmony with each other. The one is called the *cerebrum*, which lies in the front part of the skull, occupying the greater portion of its cavity; and the other is called the *cerebellum*, and occupies the back portion of the skull.

The front brain is perfect by itself, having its two hemispheres, and also its lobes. It is double, and is the organ of all *voluntary motion*, by which alone we move the head, the hands, the feet, or the whole body. This front brain is the residence, the earthly house of that part of the mind that exercises *volition*, *thought*, *understanding*, and *reason*. If one-half of this brain be paralyzed, it renders half of the system useless, so that we are unable to move it.

The back brain is also perfect by itself, having its own distinct lobes, is likewise double, and is the organ of *involuntary motion* and organic life. It throbs the heart, moves the blood, gives power to the stomach to digest its food, and imparts energy to the glands to produce their secretions. It is the residence, the earthly house of that part of the mind that exercises involuntary power in accordance with the harmony of the universe. It moves, it rolls on with external nature, drinks in, and feels her impressions, and scans them by the power of its own intuitions. This part of the mind contains all the instincts of our nature. Hence it does not *will*, *understand*, and *reason*, as the voluntary department of the mind in the front brain reasons. It intuitively knows, or *involuntarily reasons*. Under certain circumstances and conditions, like the mesmeric or psychological state, it takes the throne, compels reason to bow to its mandate, and with the brightness of its blaze throws all the voluntary powers of the soul, residing in the front brain, into comparative darkness, and pours out the eloquence of truth like a river of life, clear as crystal, from its throne. When the back brain is thus roused into action, the front brain knows nothing of its secret doings, its intuitive powers, and instinctive energies. Each brain may manifest its intelligence and impressions separate and independent, as it were, of the other, yet there is, at the same time, an undisturbed harmony, a sympathetic connection existing between the two. The *first* manifests itself by the involuntary power of *thought* and *reason.* The *second* manifests itself by the involuntary power of *intuition* and *instinct,* and while doing so, the *first* has no remembrance, no knowledge of its acts. This is a state well-known to medical men and physiological writers, who call it DOUBLE CONSCIOUSNESS. Please to bear in mind that the brain is *double,* as a meet tabernacle adapted to the living spirit or *mind* as its inhabitant, which is also *double.* Seeing, hearing, feeling, taste, and smell, are involuntary. If our eyes are open, we cannot avoid seeing; if there is a sound near us, we cannot avoid hearing; and if there is an odor, we cannot avoid smelling. As our senses are involuntary, so they belong to the involuntary power. Hence all impressions, received through the senses, are first conveyed to the involuntary department of the mind in the back brain as the grand magazine—the kitchen—where they are prepared, and then passed on to the fields of volition, thought, and reason, in the front brain, to be digested and manufactured into ideas by the power of association."

Mr. Dods applies his theory to a writing medium in this wise:

"The medium, for instance, sits down and resigns all power over the voluntary nerves, under the impression that some immortal spirit will move the hand to write, and thus make some communication through him. He assumes a state of entire passivity, and, so far as the motion of his hand is concerned, he remains perfectly indifferent. He does not *will* nor exercise even the slightest mental effort to move his hand. But soon the hand does move, either more slowly or with far more than ordinary rapidity, and a sentence is produced. But, in the production of this sentence the medium, really and honestly, had no more conscious volition than any other person present.

"How, then, it may be asked, did he form letters without thinking? The answer is, that it was *intuitively* produced by the involuntary powers of the mind, through the nervous force of the arm, and by a nervous sympathy they would produce such letters only, as by long-established habit he had uniformly written by the voluntary powers of his mind."

The sum of Mr. Dods' theory is, that "The so-called spirit-manifestations are produced by the involuntary powers of the human mind through the nervous force of *those persons only* who are either in the *electro-psychological state*, or in the *mesmeric state*, or in an entire or partial *cataleptic state*—these *three*. These three conditions, it is to be understood, involve not only somnambulism and trance, but every abnormal condition to which human beings may be subject."

CHAPTER VI.

A LITTLE PHILOSOPHY AND SOME ILLUSTRATION OF SPIRIT LANGUAGE, LITERATURE AND TACTICS.

WE shall again let an English writer on spiritualism rap for us, in this chapter, as it is our design to give to the reader as complete a view of this subject as possible. The English writer raps philosophically and illustratively as follows:

The "modern mystery" no doubt comprehends the whole phenomena of clairvoyance, magnetism, spirit-rapping, table-turning, and spectral illusions in every form. How are these produced? Whence arise they? Are they real or illusive? Are they the offspring of as yet unexplored natural laws, or are they the genuine product of deception and credulity? Let it not be unremarked either, that the believers are few, the disciples limited, or the secret in a nutshell—facts which three-fourths of the world overlook.

The normal condition of man is that of full and abundant health—health of body and of mind—*mens sana in corpore sano.* The opposite to this is disease, not of the incidental and usual kind, but organic and chronic. The functions disturbed, the tension of nerve and muscle relaxed, the cerebral system deranged, the stomach abnormal, and as it were, teeming with vapors that wrap up and blind the senses, like the phantasma of sleep, all these prepare an individual to think differently from all other people; to see in a shadowy manner; to receive strange and fantastic impressions, and to be affected by them. They are subject to electric and magnetic currents; and the fluids testify their presence in ways now so well known, that only the rarity and isolation of such abnormal cases render them comparative mysteries to the uninitiated, *i. e.* to the great body of the community. Insanity, in its mild forms of dementia and hallucination, is but another of the modes of this abnormal development. The brain-struck, the dupe of an exaggerated nervous temperament, believes as firmly in the fancies that beset him—vague, shadowy, and unreal as they are—as firmly as sanity believes in substance, weight, proportion. The demented milliner in Bedlam, waving her sceptre of straw, is as veritable to herself as ever was the Queen of Sheba, or even Victoria. These are suggestive enough of agencies acted upon by laws, chemical and organic, but also occult and unknown. What is our inference, then? Are the diseased, the nervous, the insane, to form, in their moral aspects and condition, such precedents and laws which, taken for granted, shall rule the universe, man and nature, or are they simply exceptions, showing to us that things out of their common proportion, "like sweet bells jingled out of tune," make a discord at once hideous and revolting in the sublimely harmonious working of the great universe, animate and inanimate?

These things occurring, however, where knowledge is rare, and science vague, fall under the observation of fraud and cunning. Some "medium" starts forth, and translates words and actions to the wondering crowds; and the process of imposture thus begun, continues to accelerate, like a ball rolling down hill, till the surrounding masses are leavened with fear, and awed with a "blind belief in divinities," like the superstitious man of Theophrastus. There is a principle of epidemic in whatever verges on the supernatural; and the very fact that there is an absence of all reasoning, a negation of all judgment, and an implicit and unquestioning dependence on the part of witnesses and hearers, only aid in the propaganda—fruitful as it is in all those moral evils which accrue to the world when deception is rampant, and credulity dominant.

Now belief, to be effective, should have the sanction of the larger number. Whatever can carry conviction, must arise from a vast unity of opinion. That the "mystery of the day," starting first with a diseased condition of body and of mind, should have attracted so great a degree of attention, is the more to be wondered at, when we remark, how limited, after all, its sphere is, how few, comparatively speaking, the electrical agents, the odylic bodies, are. The magneto-dynamic forces appear to affect, here and there, a few solitary individuals; but as this furnishes a stock-in-trade to the "thirty thousand *media*" of the United States, it is a justifiable inference, that where there may exist a little truth, as connected with nervous patients, and persons highly obnoxious to electrical influences, there must also be a vast deal of cheatery and imposture practised among these same thirty thousand, to make so small an amount of wares go so far.

A gloomy cast of thought generates the same tenebrous fancies. A febrile constitution is creative and fertile in imaginings. What visions, what rappings, what converse with the shadowy spectres of another existence, what communings with the radiant Æons, or what ravings with demoniac images flitting like lost souls on the Plutonian shores, when a vicious life, and intemperance, has deranged the fine corporeity of matter and spirit, all these have and hold, the doctor, the nurse, the watcher by the sick-bed, know full well. Was the communion of Socrates and his demon *all* fiction? Did Swedenborg, in his rapt ecstasies, merely weave a tissue of falsehood? Have we not some faint, vague idea, all of us, that in sleep the soul has consciousness of another life, of dwelling with other essences, of "spheres," "zones," and "circles," as the priesthood of spirit-rapping phrase it? If we do concede to the theorizers very much that may go to establish the audacious claims they make, it is because we too know, that "there are more things in heaven and earth than are dreamt of in *any* philosophy." What then? That which they term supernatural, we claim to be natural, the invariable result arising from the same invariable causes. Did the modern Psychopannichists ever draw more marvellous utterances from the spectral lips they would have us believe in, than are gathered from the lips of fever, or from a raving poet's rhapsodies? When Coleridge was under the influence of opium (which is far more marvellous in its working, than the vulgarities of table-turning,) he wrote a wondrous piece of melody, without meaning, known as "Khubla Khan." Is there more meaning derivable from darkened rooms, where electric fires flash to and fro, from furniture overthrown, from a discord of horrible noises, or from the laughable replies given to questions, spelt in defiance of grammar, and spoken without logic, which *trance* after *trance* have eliminated?

To show how easy it is to arrive at darkness from light, to convert the common-place into the mysterious, and to ally disease with the demon, we could give examples enough. It is not against the *data*, but with the *deduction*, that we must protest. It is because the world take the initiative from the impudent assertion of the mesmeric or spirit-rapping quack, and asks not, or judges not for itself, that we feel our way cautiously in this dark labyrinth. We do not laugh or scorn men's hallucinations, knowing well how easily impressions, bright or black, are made. Here for instance, is a case in point, extracted from Mrs. Crowe's remarkable work, "The Nightside of Nature."

"Dr. Bardili had a case in the year 1830, which he considered decidedly to be one of possession. The patient was a peasant woman, aged thirty-four, who never had any sickness whatever, and the whole of whose bodily functions continued perfectly regular, whilst she exhibited the following strange phenomena. She was happily married, had three children, was not a fanatic, and bore an excellent character for regularity and industry, when, without any warning or perceptible cause, she was seized with the most extraordinary convulsions, whilst a *strange* voice proceeded from her, which assumed to be that of an unblessed spirit, who had formerly inhabited a human form. While these fits were on, she entirely lost her own individuality, and became this person. On returning to herself, her understanding and character were as entire as before. The blasphemy and cursing, and barking and screeching, were dreadful. She was wounded and injured severely, by the violent falls and blows she gave herself; and when she had an intermission, she could do nothing but weep over what they told her had passed, and the state in which she saw herself. She was reduced to a skeleton; for when she wanted to eat, the spoon was turned round in her hand, and she often fasted for days together. This affliction lasted for three years, all remedies failed, and the only alleviation she obtained, was by the continued and earnest prayers of those about her, and her own; for although this demon did not like prayers, and violently opposed her kneeling down, often forcing her to outrageous fits of laughter, still they had a power over him. It is remarkable that pregnancy, confinement, and the nursing of the child, made not the least difference in her condition. * * * * At length, being magnetized, she fell into a partially somnambulic state, in which another voice was heard to proceed from her, being that of her protecting spirit, which encouraged her to patience and hope, and promised that the evil guest would be obliged to vacate his quarters. She often fell now into a magnetic state, without the aid of a magnetizer. At the end of three years, she was entirely relieved, and as well as ever.

What would the medium have made of *this?* Would he not take her ravings as invocations, and knowing the nature of a paroxysm, and its occurrences, would he not suit his subject or his question to the crisis and the hour? Or would he not give strong local coloring to what was thus uttered, and skilfully adapt such to the impressionability of his audience or hearers?

When spirit-rapping had established itself both in theory and practice, after so many years of slumber, it was found that, while being tedious, though startling perhaps, it was empty and very limited. The following, for instance, while it embodies the whole essentials of spirit-rapping, its origin, range and characteristics, shows also, as we shall presently see, that large as was its scope and action, and wonderful as it might seem, it was also as equivocal as it was insufficient for all purposes. Mr. Hammond, a clergyman, of Rochester, (U. S.,) details the particulars of a *third* visit paid to a family (the Foxes,) in whose residence the mysterious sounds we now refer to, had been heard. He says:

"I was selected from half a dozen gentlemen, and directed by these sounds to retire to another apartment, in company with the 'three sisters' and their aged mother. It was about eight o'clock in the evening. A lighted candle was placed on a large table, and we seated ourselves around it. I occupied one side of the table, the mother and youngest daughter the right, and two of the sisters the left, leaving the opposite side of the table vacant. On taking our position, the sounds were heard, and continued to multiply and become more violent, until every part of the room trembled with their demonstrations. They were unlike anything I had heard before. Suddenly, as we were all resting on the table, I felt the side next to me move upward. I pressed upon it heavily, but soon it passed out of the reach of us all, full six feet from me, and at least four from the person nearest to it. * * * In this position it was situated when the question was asked, 'Will the spirit move the table back where it was before?' And back it came, as though it were carried on the head of some one who had not suited his position to a perfect equipoise, the balance being sometimes in favor of one side, and then the other. But it regained its first position. In the meantime the demonstrations grew louder and louder. The family commenced and sung the 'spirit's song,' and several other pieces of *sacred* music, during which accurate time was marked on the table, causing it to vibrate; a transparent hand, resembling a shadow, presented itself before my face. I felt fingers taking hold of a lock of hair, on the left side of my head, causing an inclination of several inches, then a cold-death-like hand was drawn designedly over my face, three gentle raps over my left knee, my right limb forcibly pulled against strong resistance, under the table, a violent shaking, as though two hands were applied to my shoulders, myself and chair uplifted, and moved back, and several slaps as with the hand on the sides of the head, which were repeated on each one of the company. During these manifestations, a piece of pasteboard, nearly a foot square, was swung with such velocity before us, as to throw a strong current of air into our faces, a paper curtain attached to one of the windows, was rolled up and unrolled twice, a lounge immediately behind me was shaken violently. Two small drawers in a bureau played back and forth with inconceivable rapidity; a sound resembling a man sawing boards, and planing them, was heard under the table; a common spinning-wheel seemed to be in motion, making a very natural buzz of the spindle; a reel articulated each knot wound upon it, while the sound of a rocking cradle indicated maternal cares for the infant's slumbers. I felt a perfect self-possession, except a momentary chill when the cold hand was applied to my face, similar to a sensation I have realized when touching a dead body."

And now let us see how "spirit-rapping," under the judicious training of its media, created for itself new methods of development, and rendered the business of the medium more complicated. Between the souls of the living and those departed, we will assume, from the solemn yearnings, the promises of dwelling together in a future state, and from a number of other indications of a like nature, that, if there be no *direct* communion, there is ground to believe the *wish* for it exists. Now, if whatever difficulties lie in the way, be removed—if there arises one who can stand between, and interpret the question and the answer, tell the desire, and make known the revelation, the desideratum has at once its accomplishment. Whether we believe the fact or no, such persons have asserted themselves. The spirits are not to be controlled by the medium, though it would seem that they are sensible to entreaty, and that an excess of politeness is never thrown away. The medium cannot command a presence, nor if there be a presence, can he compel its (alleged) usual mode of signifying that it—that is, the spirit—is there.

Now, the alphabetical order of rapping is not only well known, but its tediousness has been experienced and commented upon in many a daily journal. The progress made in this round-about manner, gives some 240 letters in an hour. Consequently, as the method is diffuse, and time is exhausted, the most momentous revelations—none of the remotest consequences have as yet been recorded—can never be made, unless the communion can, like chapters in a serial, be "continued in our next." A sort of oral short-hand would have been desirable, only that the thing would be so full of breaks and incoherences, as to render *that* impossible.

Philosophy resolves many difficulties. Perseverance conquers all obstacles. The proper study of the medium was spirit, and he ingeniously constructed a card, with the letters of the alphabet upon it, as an experiment, to be laid aside if it failed. We know not what we can do, like the Hibernian with the double-bass, till we try.

During a communication between the medium and the supposed spirit, the former passed his hand over the alphabet, until he found his finger sensibly and irresistibly arrested at a certain letter, and so on, until the word, the sentence, was completed. What sort of communications these turned out to be, read all the works published on the subject, and—laugh.

The hand of the medium is thus calmly given over to the devices of the "spirit." This chronic power extends over its brawn and muscle, without aught that we know of intervening between. Sometimes it is mild and gentle—sometimes violent and rude. At others it hesitates, and the digit hovers in suspense over the magic letters. These letters are spelt with immense rapidity for the most part, and the words, as spelt, are called out; and it is said that an expert penman would be puzzled to follow the dictation, when the "steam" is really on. To this system there arose many very serious objections; besides that, the revelations made through two mediums contradicted each other very flatly.

In this *modus operandi* of the revelation there was yet a hitch. Improved as the system was, it yet failed, after having worked well for a time, to satisfy the avidity of the curious. It was but a small difficulty to obviate, the trouble of being, in a manner, one's own decipherer. The same influence that could leave the sphere, through odylic attraction, with the medium, and compel his hand to spell a meaning and a phrase, could dismiss the more cumbrous machinery, and make the same hand write for itself. *C'est un fait accompli.* The thing was done; but no sooner had one written on this hint, than a score of writing mediums, like so many Richmonds, were in the field.

As credulity enlarged itself, in some degree, it must have puzzled the mediums to keep pace with its march. It was a bold hazard to urge a belief upon audience after audience, who assemble to behold a man sitting at a table to write, that he did this with an abnegation of self, with a negation of all will, and that what resulted, was the effect of a plenary and spiritual inspiration. They explained its mysteries thus :—The spirit gave the medium mind and hand. One is paralyzed for the moment—the other is active. The hand thus active, is active only by the spirit power which urges it. There is a discrepancy about the manner in which this power is used, whether internal—by volition of electric currents through the muscular tissue—or by a sort of dominant but unseen outer force. In these things simplicity and plainness would lose their effect, and the result of a statement, simply and lucidly made, would have provoked laughter and scorn.

What wonder, then—if the appetite of the curious predisposes them to believe in supernatural agencies, in second sight, clairvoyance, magnetism, and spectre-seeing—that there should be no lack of food and provender for so rabid a taste? We know too well, that such a thing as being *en rapport* with a person can exist. Nay, it does. Is not this the whole secret of the attraction and the repulsion of life? It is the characteristic of electric phenomena to exhibit itself in noise and luminous flashes. What can this have to do with rapping, card-spelling, and the like? Even the hierophants of the system do not explain the connexion. Admitting that "spirit"-rapping be a positive actuality, where are its uses, what its tendency, and what its value? If it be portions of an unexplained phenomenon, which has not yet attained full development, how is it that, with the discovery alone, the whole of its results terminate? Without entering here into the question of its propriety—without inquiring whether it is, or is not, portion of a forbidden and unholy art, we can yet feel surprised that, with so much parade, there should be produced such imbecile consequences for any tangible good—not to speak here of those deplorable casualties which the annals of insanity or coma but too terribly point out.

The invention of a language for the spirit-spheres, was a thing that might have been earlier hit upon. It is written by the medium, but in no recognized characters, antique or modern. On the shores of ancient Nile, no sign or carven stone, no mystic tongue of the priesthood, nor Coptic letters, give the faintest foreshadowing of it. A young lady (so says the "Spiritual Telegraph") translates this undiscoverable tongue into the sounds of a short sentence, "Ki-e-lou-cou-ze-ta," and again renders this Ethiopian serenaders' burthen of a chorus, to which it seems most alike, as follows:—"As heaven or the spirit-spheres are to be the future home of all mankind, so is knowledge to accompany them in the paths of wisdom; while peace and love, in a chain of goodness, shall bind the universal whole in the bonds of harmony." A very fine phrase this—"goot 'orts loot you," as Captain Fluellen said—and proves the compressible elasticity that can comprehend some sixty round syllables within six, and is doubtless the oral short-hand we lamented the absence of some few pages back.

They have, as a part of the mode, the incantation, and the invocation. There must be incense, adulation, and poetry too. As in the spheres they have music, and musk, ambergris, fans, and fine clothes, so have the neophytes an affectation of fumigation, singing, and other modern modes of divination. To contemplate the excessive air of satisfaction with which the geographical and social details of the circles and zones are given, is a matter of pure wonderment to us, who have not the gift of singing, and whose imaginations are pitifully restricted, all we fear, of small avail. Why is it that we hear so little of spirit-rapping just now, compared to what we did a few months past? Are spirits and professors gone to "star it" elsewhere? Is the delusion on the decline, and the system fallen in speedy decadence? Has ingenuity exhausted itself, and failed to go farther? One by one the pretences have been stripped, and laid aside. Collusion has been exposed, and the machinery of a rapping-table proved an ingenious knavery. Electric shocks, and the dislocation of knee-caps, have been more than spoken of, and *Poltergeist* himself has taken sheltor in Franklin's Leyden jar.

They are not to be compared, we think, with the

marvellous verities of Doctors Kerner and Reichenbach, in the matter of Angélique Cottin, and Frederica Hauffe. Truth is stranger than fiction, and catalepsy, somnambulism, and the like, are mysteries far more awful, we believe, than spirit-rapping, or any of the communications that have descended from any sphere. Between knowledge and ignorance, a strong race is running; and whether this is to be an age of credulity and imposture, or one of calm inquiry, where doubt itself holds a reverend air, and skepticism shrinks abashed, as yet remains to be seen. Meantime, let us proceed with our investigation of the mystery.

While considering the claims of the spirit-rappists, in every possible way, and giving them ungrudgingly all the advantages they can *prove*, and even more, the fact must not be overlooked, that all the marvel, the wonder, the astounding part of spirit-rapping, and its congeners, lie *less* in its *de facto* existence, and literal aspects, than in the prose-poetical coloring which the *littérateurs* of that doctrine have presented to an admiring, and let us hope, (or their labor is else thrown away) a grateful world. To read the writings of Adin Ballou, and of the spirit journals, gazettes, and other spectral bulletins of the States, is like reading a new revelation. The story of Cupid and Psyche—the splendid fables of old mythology—the gorgeous habiliments of the Arabian Nights, all pale "their ineffectual fires" before the glories thus indicated to our mundane eyes. Mystery is the arch enchantress in all things, material and immaterial; and so Zoroaster taught that fire was the principle of life, and mounts upward to meet its lord and master; and Plato peopled space with a teeming mass of breathing creatures, the minute atoms of an invisible universe, surrounding and pervading even us. So also, according to the fanciful jargon of the old Platonic schools, fire, air, and water, owe their origin to the principle of the scalene triangle; that the earth is created from the principle of right-angled triangles; that sphere and pyramid symbolize in themselves the *figure* of flame; while air is figured in the octahedron, and water by the icosahedron, and the like; that the sphere images the beautiful and the true, as containing and comprehending all things and principles that are or can be suggested by geometric formulæ. Now, carrying out this principle of mystery, it is easy to understand the solemnities of the Eleusinian mysteries; the fulgid splendors, playing in keen and darting fires, as the great veil that separated the neophyte from the hierophant, in the Temple of Isis (the mysteries of knowledge only being foreshadowed); the sphinx-like riddle of the Coptic Zodiac, so easy of solution, being a meteorological alphabet of the seasons, better explained in symbol and hieroglyph than by any other known method. It is easy to comprehend the thirst to know, the awe with which the ardent approached such lofty secrets as these, and how Delphic Apollo, Dodonian Oak, Ephesian Diana, and Roman Sybil became, in the eyes of the unlearned world, the august impersonations, and the incarnations of mystery, which in fact they were.

It has been thus through every age downward. The

human mind is the same. Its senses, passions, and extremes of belief and doubt, precisely the same, only that the conditions are changed. We now learn for ourselves, and trust little to tradition. The experiences of past errors warn us, and that which comes to us with all the pretence of a mystery about it, we gaze coolly enough at, however ghostly the aspect of the thing may be, and we question it, examine it, probe it, wonder at it, perhaps, and feel baffled; but we call it no mystery. Whatever it may appear to be for a time, but not for long—sooner or later we shall know it for what it is, and in another instance discover that our knowledge of the laws of natural phenomena is by no means as complete as it is desirable that it should be.

Now, it is the laws of spirit-rapping, table-turning, and intercommunion, that we are at present in doubt about. We do not deny the possibility of all these three taking place, and being among the uncommon occurrences of life; but we do not go so far as to insist upon their existence either. The due regard we owe to truth—the knowledge at least that we have of the infinite mutations, and the continued new forms of matter, fresh combinations, and still other ultimate elements, science and discovery, should deter us from anything like dogmatism, either to assert or to deny. Spirit-rapping, table-turning, and magnetism exist, and do occur without doubt—that is to say, *so called* "spirit"-rapping. Why is it necessary that this process, so ludicrous—these spirit-communications, so jejune and vague, so contradictory, and so destitute of the meanest logic—

these magnetic phenomena, and the electric affinities which are subject to the laws of the physical universe, should be attributed to supernatural interference, and have a supernatural origin? They are not a whit the more respectable, and in the majority of instances, lessen the reverence that we intuitively pay to the awful voices of the soul, when in prayer, meditation, and in dream, the eternity beyond the grave discloses its grand and imposing portals to us.

We term the best known of those forces which rule the material world, the laws of gravity, and so on, by the word physical. It may mean nothing direct, but it implies all. Like the great Pan, it is the comprehension of all that is scientific, natural, and in accordance with all human experience, from the days of the Deluge and onwards. Chemical forces, those of light, caloric, magnetism, all belong to the physical. Higher in the scale, and less known to the learned and the scientific, are those forces termed *vital*. Under this term, are comprehended the succession of seed-time and harvest, the ripening summer, and the vigorous winter that cleanses, preserves, and purifies the ground, and gives it those nourishing virtues which make the great bosom of nature so benign and beneficent. To this belong decay and reproduction, and with it, life and death are as the opposite poles, of a certainly most mysterious circle of procession. Beyond these relations to the vital force, are those of the brain and nerves, the phenomena of will, and the muscular volition that waits subserviently upon it. *Will* but to raise the arm, or lift the leg, and it is done. There are organic forces, too, quite independent of the will. The systole and diastole of the heart, the diffusion of oxygen through the blood by contact and absorption, the peristaltic motion, and the convulsive cramp of epilepsy, which is a derangement of the general working of these forces, are so many familiar illustrations.

Because, however, these are organic, and because they do act and work with a miraculous accuracy, for the space often of "threescore years and ten," there must be something acting on these—heart, lungs, brain, and viscera—which is equivalent to the will. What is this supplementary power then? What renders us liable to generate caloric so largely, and to become transmuted in abnormal instances into so many Leyden jars, so many gymnotic eels, unless it be that force termed by Reichenbach as Od, or Odyle—that is, allied to the nature of magnetic electricity, but regarding the sources, nature, qualities, and extent of which, the philosophers have not yet decided? The spirit-rappists have been premature in their conclusions, we think, and speaking of them and their theories, with all the respect we can muster, we would say that they had been led by their very vivid imaginations to step aside from the path of truth, unintentionally very likely, and in order to account for what was else unintelligible, settled the doctrine of spirits, spheres, and the like, and so produced the prolific results already seen, but which results we must take leave to say, are like exchanging a good golden sovereign for twenty of the most spurious shillings that ever came from the forger's crucible—and hence, saddling us with all the consequences of being duped.

In the spirit-spheres there is a progression through degrees of perfection, until the expiating spirit, gradually leaving aside its grosser weight of impurities, finally arises at the highest acme of that refulgent glory its starward aspirations are bent upon. There is nothing to quarrel with in this theory, if, as the indication very strongly points out, we are content to dispense with Scriptures, and conform to a new revelation, published in the United States, at the "Penny Celestial Spheres' Journal" office. The idea of expiation is agreeable to the sinner, supposing it to be tenable ground *after* death. On the other hand, we require better proofs, a larger amount of information than we now possess, before we can subscribe to it. Ignorance and fanaticism will always become proselytes to the most agreeable doctrine—and to do away with perdition and the pandemonium of lost souls, is the first step to win their favor; but unfortunately, we cannot annihilate St. Paul's by denying its existence, or proving in the Aristotelian fashion, that it never was erected.

We learn from old writers, through the pages of Gibbon and others, that the monks of Mount Athos had a singular method of throwing themselves into ecstatic trances, of dreaming dreams, and dwelling in the bosom of an hallucination that unfolded them like a glory. When alone in the cell, they closed the door, and seating themselves apart, sought to raise the mind above all things vain and transitory. Reclining beard and chin on the breast, and turning eyes and thoughts to the region of the navel, they sought there for the seat of the soul. At first, all was comfortless and dark; but perseverance brought by degrees an ineffable joy, and no sooner had the soul discovered the place of the heart, than it was involved in a mystic and ethereal light. On this account, those harmless ascetics obtained the name of Quietists, till their idiosyncracies were scattered to the winds by edicts and violent hands. Anarchy displaced *Estatica*, and the soul became troubled and dark. This mystic and ethereal light we should add, was asserted, and believed to be synonymous with the luminous transfiguration on Mount Tabor.

The crystal, the drop of water, the fixing of the eyes upon an object so long that there ensued a certain temporary derangement of the nervous organs, is so evidently allied with, and the clear precursor of, animal magnetism, that no arguments seem necessary to prove the intimacy of the connection. Jamblichus, who was the theosophist of the Platonic doctrines, bears apt testimony to the alleged divine *afflatus* pervading the enthusiast.

"Man," he says, "has a double life, one annexed to the body, the other separate from everything bodily. * * * * In sleep we have the capacity of being wholly loosed from the chains that confine our spirit, and can make use of the life which is not dependent on generation. When the soul is thus separate from the body in sleep, then that (latter) kind of life which usually remains separable and separate by itself, immediately awakes within us, and acts according to its proper nature, * and in that state has a presaging knowledge of the future." Then, omitting a distinction between sleeping and waking inspiration, and coming to the latter, in which, also, the *afflati* have a presaging power, he proceeds:—"Yet those (latter) are so far awake that they can use their senses, yet are not capable of reasoning; * * * for they neither (properly speaking) sleep when they seem to do so, nor awake when they seem awake; for they do not of themselves foresee, nor are they moved by any human instrumentality; neither know they their own condition; nor do they exert any prerogative or motion of their own; but all this is done under the power and by the energy of the deity. For that they who are so affected, do not live an ordinary animal life, is plain, because many of them, on contact with fire, are not burnt, the divine inward afflatus repelling the heat; or, if they be burnt, they do not feel it; neither do they feel prickings, or scratchings, or other tortures. Further, that their actions are not (merely) human, is apparent from this, that they make their way through pathless tracts, and pass harmless through the fire, and pass over rivers in a wonderful manner, which the priestess herself also does in the Cataballa. By this it is plain that the life they live, is not human, nor animal, nor dependent on the use of senses, but divine, as if the soul were taking its rest, and the deity were there instead of the soul. Various sorts there are of those so divinely inspired, as well by reason of the varying divinity of the inspiring gods as of the modes of inspiration. These modes are of this sort, either the deity occupies us, or we join ourselves to the deity, &c. * * * According to these diversities, there are different signs, effects, and works of the inspired; thus, some will be moved in their whole bodies, others in particular members—others again, will be motionless. Also, they will perform *dances and chants*, some well, some ill. The bodies again, of some, will seem to dilate in height, of others in compass; and others again, will seem to walk in air." To be insensible to pains, prickings, shakings, &c., is to be in that condition so familiar to us all when a patient is seized with convulsions, cramp, epilepsy and the like, and the frenzy of inspired dancing, are as well known to the scholar who has read of the Corybantes, the Mænades, and the Bacchic rites, as to the young, who have read of David in a sacred *furor* dancing before the ark.

Now, the spirit-rappists scorn to be outdone by the dancing manias of the middle, and even of later ages, familiar to the readers of history. Could such an important section of spiritual, angelic, or demoniac phænomena be by any possibility omitted? As the mediums have made over to the spirits of the spheres, all the modern musical instruments in vogue, and have heard the ravishing concerts which are there held, it was but natural that those among us who were at all *en rapport* with the denizens of the spheres, should follow an example so worthily set in old traditions, and in the annals of witchcraft.

As "Rapping" was speedily superseded by the card alphabet writing, by clairvoyance, and by other forms of the spiritual presence, dancing soon followed as another phase of manifestations, and it was remarked that those affected by the spiritual impulse, illustrate the manner and the individuality of a deceased person so faithfully, that those acquainted with the departed, recognize the person at once. All this is very pitiful—for, admitting the whole to be true, from the spirit down to the dancer, through every grade and agency, what satisfies us? what good, what benefit, present or to come, are we likely to obtain?

One locality of the States can boast of a hundred persons who have been thus influenced. They comprise persons of all ages. They must have music too, and the strains of Strauss or Jullien give animation to the dances thus said to be impromptued. Is it not gratuitous, however, to attribute anything here to the spirits? Where is the difference, we should like to know, between the dancing of one assembly where the spirit *is*, and of another where the spirit is *not?* Possibly the spirit-dance is known by its eccentricity, its movements as often graceful as ungainly. "Eccentric" is the word used to express the same. There were impure dances in pagan times, as in the early days of Christianity—so its vilifiers wrote it down. There was the Witch Sabbath of the Brocken, where dances under baleful mastery were held. Pass to-day through some Hindoo jungle into the sacred space where the temple stands, and there they yet hold their orgiac dances. The horrible obscenities of the New Zealand dances in their Morai are on record. What do they say of the low *salles* of Paris, and the *cancan*, whose repute is more than enough—what of the casinos of London? What amount of seduction is required to ally impurity with delusion, vice with ignorance, and the strong ruling hand of knowing cheatery and guile, when it has such plastic material to work upon as the gullibility of the public, as well as its heedlessness, and its insatiate appetite for novelty in any form?

These dances we hold then to be among the most equivocal portion of spiritual manifestations we know of. Analogies from the same cause and effect, deductions from the same veritable premises, are *never* wrong. The very inclination to be contradictory, is proof of the rule, and of our assertion. We do not accuse these people of erecting schools for crime; but why do they or their spirits make such an easy peace between evil lives, and a lenient future—nay, a perfect "happy land"—as they do? Is it from conviction? Human hardihood, even with a knowledge of the laws of the Creator, can live, and *has* lived a life of profligacy and crime, has even "cursed God and died!" Are we to learn now that a knowledge of the moral and religious laws hinder a man from being the high priest, the hierarch, the tutor and the teacher of vice? To the plausibility of the "spirit-rappists" is added a great deal of shallowness. We must not permit systematic vice to become an adjunct to immoral growth, even if we are premature, in being doubtful and suspicious.

We must, however, return awhile, in order to examine as closely as possible the analogies that may exist between the od or electro-magnetic force, and the so-called spiritual influences, and whether the one is not easily convertible into the other, the mysterious giving way to that, which if not thoroughly known, will not so far elude us, but that study, experiment, and minutest examination may disclose all that as yet remains hidden.

It is held that the forces are visible and invisible; they are also voluntary and involuntary—and while the voluntary forces are, in a greater or less degree, under cognizance, the involuntary are not, and hence it is that their working constitutes a mystery; the occult powers that influence them, belong to the phenomena of the unknown, and as a corollary when seeking to know their nature, we either give up the search, or assign it to "spirit-manifestations" at once, and so for ever settle the difficulty by a designation it does not define. We act rashly and illogically, thus to establish an evil precedent which bolder theorists take advantage of, and so erect a cumbrous and unwieldy edifice of superstition, which becomes finally more confounding than the multitudinous incarnations of Vishnu, or the myriad-sided forms under which Hindoo mythology seeks to speak to man.

Desiring, however, to obtain some insight into those vital forces which move tables, chairs, &c., and induce coma and the like, and which are so closely allied to the productive principle of life, we ascend to loftier grounds of inquiry, and on all sides around us the horizon enlarges itself. Experiment proves that the vital force which gives rise to a rotatory or progressive motion in an inert body, has some reference to the electrical conditions of the agent that acts, and the factor that transfers the energy from the person to the substance. There is in the turning of the table, an unconscious muscular action, without doubt, exercised. This unconscious muscular action has a tendency, like all motion gravitating round a centre, to be circular in its operations, such as we observe in the tendrils of certain plants, whose magnetic affinities with light and heat, may have a common origin with those of the vital force referred to. We observe singular instances of a vital and involuntary force actively at work in persons who have received a sudden injury. Shot through the heart, a man has made a convulsive leap he could not otherwise have accomplished. Animals struck at the region of the brain, have spun round and round. The paroxysms of insanity, while being perfectly involuntary, indicate an accession of the vital force equivalent to that possessed by four or six robust men in a normal state of physical health. Is it to be wondered that under a condition (nervously) familiar to us, the energy of this power, as in the battery of animated hands laid on the table, should exhibit latent forces and unknown powers never before dreamed of, and flow in a plenteous magnetic current through the fingers, and that four or six persons, whose united strength, *voluntarily* exercised, would not have sufficed to move a table, should yet *in*voluntarily compel it to whirl, and to move onwards, as though it were a toy in a child's hand?

It is to the delicate experiments and to the persevering course of observations undertaken by Reichenbach, that we are chiefly indebted for having thrown some light on the subject, by his theory of the Od force. It is to this theory of a resistless current—an invisible, but extraordinary agency, which is not electricity, nor magnetism, but which partakes more of the character of the latter than of the former—that we may assign the origin of the involuntary and "vital" forces which have puzzled more than the "spirit-rappists' themselves. Who would suppose that in experiments made upon the magnetic currents of the muscles, this (Od) agent, while playing among the rain-drops of a summer's day, can shake the earth and the very heavens?" Whoever imagines that because Reichenbach was not capable of such mastery over his discovery, as that of showing his "Od" capable of making a table dance, it is not after all the said Od that does it? It is not always clear that analogy and fact are seen in all their integrity and value. Odic smoke or ether, can be made to play luminously on the *surface* of bodies, but he must be a bad arguer, and know little of the theory of atoms and the porosity of the most concrete substances, that will assert this ether to be incapable of mingling with matter and thoroughly permeating it. Trivial discrepancies can only modify to superficial eyes the fundamental facts, just as exceptions prove a rule. If we have at the least got a clue to natural phenomena that may dispense with spiritual agency, let us make the best of *that* as more consonant with reason. The palpable may glide into the impalpable by such gradations as have no discernible line of demarcation; but they are connected and related, as the brain to the brawn, the will to the deed, the soul to the body.

The literature of spirit-rapping, table-moving, and the like, is not the least curious part of the matter under debate. While it appears steadily to ignore mere vulgar matter, so many corroborative, as well as correlative ties of relationship peep out now and then, as clearly show a lack of decision, and a latitude of allowance. The very fact that spirits meddle in what we may term the hucksterings of our physical tax-paying, bread-earning existence, shows some such contact with the material that is, to say the least of it, suspicious, and calculated to throw doubts upon the intact impalpability spirits may lay claim to.

In closing this chapter, we cannot, we think, do better than to give our readers a specimen of this strange literature, and of the logic of the "spirit-world." The work "Light from the Spirit-world," (of course, of American origin, to "go a-head," after the most consistent fashion,) is asserted to be written without the exercise of will or volition of any kind. The medium did no more than submit himself to the *afflatus*, or the influence of the spirit he was in communication with. The hand was surrendered to the spirits, the will was suspended, and the medium became an automaton for the time. It is professed to have been published without alteration or correction of any kind. This we will implicitly credit; for the following specimen of spirit-eloquence satisfies us that in many respects, especially those of composition, meaning, and grammar, the mortal is immeasurably superior to his shadowy kindred in the spheres. Here, then, is a luminous exposition of the spiritual idea of wisdom, the premises, argument, and corollary of which we should be very glad to see contravened, if there exist one daring enough to venture on the desperate attempt of challenging a spirit on his own ground:

"Wisdom is wisdom. All is not wisdom. All is not folly. Wisdom wills good. Folly wills otherwise. One is right. One is wrong. Wisdom will do right. Folly will do wrong. He that is wise, let him take heed. He who is unwise, let him get wisdom. And let him get it where it is to be found. Let him not seek for it in the folly of fools, but in men of understanding—in spirits commissioned by God, to give light to those who grope in darkness. Let him cast off the shackles, tear asunder the false robes, rend the galling chains, and burst the bonds that enslave his captive soul. Let him launch his mind into the stream of wisdom flowing from the fountain of God, and bathe in the limpid waters, that he may be healed.

"Wisdom is not selfish. Wisdom is not partial. Human wisdom is both. Men are considered wise, but their wisdom is comparatively foolishness. Men are wise only as they gain knowledge. Men are unwise when they neglect what they need to make them wise. Men are wise when they do good—unwise when they do evil. Men are wise in what they know—unwise in what they do not know. Knowledge of God is wisdom. Knowledge is power. Knowledge is good. Knowledge will save. Knowledge will cure. Knowledge will do what ignorance cannot do. Hence knowledge of God, is the wisdom of God, the power of God, and the goodness of God. Neither could wisdom exist without God."—*Light from the Spirit-world*, pp. 39, 40.

The names of Paine, the truculent, Calvin, the uncompromising, Edgar Poe, the poet, whose genius was so brilliantly erratic, and whose great talents were obscured, alas! by degrading vices, of Washington, of Franklin, of Adam Clarke, and of others, occur plentifully as dictating dispatches from the spirit-world. A strong current of worldly wisdom and the craft of the earthly wise, run through them. They savor of self-interest, and are as transparent as the Visions of Mahomet, who in trance beheld what he wanted ordered for him by the fiat of Gabriel, or any other handy *deus ex machinâ*—or precisely in the same manner that the Mormon leaders have the *nous* to assign for their own uses, through prophetic revelation, the choicest goods of the community, the high places of life, and all the advantages that can accrue to cunning, when it has elaborated itself into a system, and asserts mastery over blind belief, ignorance and error.

One more extract from these spirit-metaphysics, and we enter upon another part of the subject. The "Mind" is the theme thus loftily descanted upon:

The noble powers of mind, how much debased to the production of thought bemeaning to its purposed dignity!

"Mind, the quickening principle of which originates in God, and is designed to range the majestic universe, to gather strength from every dropping sand within its sphere—from the contemplation of every moving atom in the vastness of unmeasured space—from the animating principle of every living thing—from the lote and mollusca, through the ascending degree of higher life and expanding intellectually, to the flaming seraph who attends the Creator at his throne—in man is wounded by the deadly and demoralizing nature of sin against goodness, and is thus prevented its lofty ascent; and, being impelled in pursuit of fancy pearl by the motive force of evil, is rendered a penal slave to vice, prejudice, and vain ambitious life. Hence, from its secret chambers is poured forth a chaotic mass of garbled vindictive imprecations, terminating in oppressions, ambitious cruelties, and the catalogue indicative of a mind in perfect wreck, driven and dashed against the fatal rocks that rend in sunder the noble form and despoil the garnished soul of the human body.

"Mind, designed to harmonize in its own movements, and in ascension wing its way through portals of wisdom, bearing along by attraction the weaker elements around, is crushed and welters in gore at the base of the mountain of sin, and tending to the dark abyss, drags with it that embraced by the power of its influence."

Do you not admire all this, good reader? Are you quite insensible to the taste, the propriety, the prose-poetry of these ambitious sentences? It must have been a love of hard words and sounding syllables alone that could not content itself with simple expressions, conveying a simple meaning. But what would you? If spirits do speak or dictate, we cannot expect them to indite, or otherwise act like your mere mortal. What, in that case, would their superiority consist in?

CHAPTER VII.

ANCIENT RAPPERS, TABLE-TIPPERS, AND SPEAKING MEDIUMS.

In this chapter we shall give the reader a peep into the antiquity of Spiritual Rappers. By "Rappers," we mean of course, every phase of modern spiritualism, such as rapping, tipping, and speaking under entrancement.

In ancient Greece, centuries on centuries ago, there was a magnificent temple at Delphi, built over the sacred well of Cassotis, which was supposed to emit an entrancing vapor, which inspired those who inhaled it, with prophetic inspiration. In the centre of this temple was a golden statue of Apollo, before which was an altar on which there always burned a fire of firwood and laurel leaves. Before the altar was the sacred well, and over the well was a tripod. This temple, with its statue, its sacred well, its altar and its tripod, was the seat of the most famous oracle of Greece. The priestess of the oracle, when the same was consulted, crowned her head with laurel, seated herself on the tripod, inhaled the vapor from the sacred well, and was seized at once with a fit, as modern spiritualists would call it, of entrancement. Her face changed color, her limbs were violently convulsed, and with howlings and disjointed sentences, she spoke the oracle, gave to those, who asked, an answer to their inquiries, which was received by them as a voice from another world. In other words, she was, in the language of modern spiritualists, a speaking medium, through which immortals were supposed to communicate to mortals. This is the oldest form, by way of entrancement, of modern Spirit Rapping.

Next comes a voice from the middle of the third century, about A. D. 250. Tertullian, one of the fathers of the church, who wrote about this period, says:

"Do not your magicians call ghosts and departed souls from the shades below, and by their infernal charms, represent an infinite number of delusions? And how do they perform all this, but by the assistance of evil angels and demons, by which they are able to MAKE STOOLS AND TABLES PROPHESY?"

This is the first mention made of table-tipping.

The next, in order of time, is a table-turning development, the date of the occurrence of which is about A. D. 360. At the time we refer to, Valens was Emperor of Rome, and he consulted two soothsayers, as they were then called. In the centre of the room where the consultation took place, there stood a three-legged table, made of laurel-wood. The table was covered with a cloth, on the edge of which the letters of the alphabet were marked, and over the centre of the table a metallic ring was suspended. Two men named Patricius and Hillarius, officiated on the occasion. Valens asked who would be the next emperor. The table tipped, the ring vibrated, and the letters over which the ring rested the longest, were spelt out, as T. H. E. O. D. Valens left the circle and put every one in his dominions to death, whom he could find, whose name began with T. H. E. O. D. Theodosius, however, was the next emperor who ascended the throne. This is the only account of table-tipping which we can find, and it is recorded in the *Rerum Gestarum* of Ammianus Marcellinus, page 552, Paris edition, 1681.

Next follows, in point of time, a rapping development. Rushton Hall, in Northamptonshire, England, was long the residence of a family by the name of Tresham. In the reign of Queen Elizabeth, Sir Thomas Tresham occupied the mansion. He was a pedant and fanatic. At a short distance from the old Hall, there was a lodge, built by Sir Thomas, the walls of which within and without, were covered all over with emblems of the Trinity. He took this pictorial mode to illustrate his firm belief in the Trinity. About twenty years ago, there was found secreted in a wall of this old mansion, in Northamptonshire, a letter, written by Sir Thomas Tresham, and dated A. D. 1554, from which we make the following extract.

"I usually having my servants to read to me an hour after supper, it fortuned that Fulcis, my then servant, reading in the *Christian Revelation and Proof that there is a God*, there was upon the wainscot table, at that instant, three loud knocks (as if it had been an iron hammer) given, to the great amazing of me and my two servants, Fulcis and Nilkton."

This first account of rapping is, as the reader perceives, of the date 1554, three hundred years ago.

The following is of a few years' later date, about the beginning of the 17th century. It is related by Richard Baxter, in his "Historical Discourses of Apparitions," as quoted by De Foe, in his "Life of Duncan Campbell" (p. 109). The date of this occurrence, was about the middle of the 16th century. "There is now in London an understanding, sober, pious man, oft one of my hearers, who has an elder brother, a gentleman of considerable rank, who having formerly seemed pious, of late years does often fall into the sin of drunkenness; he often lodges long together here in his brother's house, and whensoever he is drunk and has slept himself sober, something knocks at his bed's head, as if one knocked on a wainscot. When they remove his bed, it follows him. Besides other loud noises on other parts where he is, that all the house hears, they have often watched him, and kept his hands lest he should do it himself. His brother has often told it to me, and brought his wife, a discreet woman, to attest it, who avers moreover, that as she watched him, she has seen his shoes under the bed taken up, and nothing visible to touch them. They brought the man himself to me, and when we asked him how he dare sin again after such a warning, he had no excuse."

We come now to another rapping development, of a still later date.

The celebrated John Wesley's family, it is notorious, was for a considerable time, subject to strange annoyances, somewhat like the sounds and rappings characteristic of the modern mystery. So serious did the great founder of Wesleyanism deem the manifestation, that he took up his pen to relate all he knew about them. The history of these noises is very briefly as follows:—In 1715, when John Wesley's father, the Rev. S. Wesley, resided in the glebe house of Epworth, in Lincolnshire, sundry curious noises were repeatedly heard by several members of the family, who carefully concealed the matter from old Wesley, lest he might think, as they thought, that these were forewarnings of his approaching death. This course could not be long continued, as the disturbances became daily greater, and more inclined to make the head of the house hear. When he did, he was rather amused than alarmed; for he considered certain young gentlemen, who were attentive to his daughters by day, meant to compliment them in that curious manner by night. The daughters, who felt persuaded that this was too pleasing a key to the puzzle, rather encouraged the good man's notion than disabused it. Once, however, it occurred that, after he went to bed, a singular tapping in the next room induced him to leap up and discover its cause; but neither then nor afterwards did he find any clue to the noise.

The children, who were at first a little, and by degrees not at all afraid, had a very decided belief that the noise was occasioned by an old man called Jeffery, who died in the house; and they were accustomed to cry, when the tappings were heard, "Here comes Jeffery," observing, "He is early" or "late to-night," as the case may be. It was not for a long time easy to convince the elder members of the family that the noise was not occasioned by some ingenious trick of the younger. In order to be quite certain, Mary, the eldest daughter, contrived to remain up once, instead of a younger sister, to remove her father's candle when he had gone to bed. John Wesley fully relates his sister's adventure :—She had no sooner taken away the candle, than she heard a noise below. She hastened down stairs to where the noise was, but it was then in the kitchen. She ran into the kitchen, where it was tapping the inside of the screen. When she went round, it was drumming on the outside; then she heard a knocking at the back kitchen door. She ran to it, unlocked it softly, and when the knocking was repeated, suddenly opened it; but nothing was to be seen. As soon as she shut it, the knocking began again. She opened it again, but could see nothing; when she turned to go to bed, the knocking recommenced and continued. " From that time," writes her brother, " she was thoroughly convinced there was no imposture in the matter."

As we have said, the family got quite accustomed to, and lost all terror in the disturbances. John Wesley, in telling us so, adds :—" A gentle tapping at the children's bed-head, usually began between nine and ten at night; they then commonly said to each other, 'Jeffery is coming; it is time to go asleep.' And if they heard a noise in the day, and said to my younger sister, 'Hark, Kizzy, Jeffery is knocking above,' she would run up stairs, and pursue it from room to room, saying she desired no better diversion."

We might go on multiplying instances of the above kind occurring about the same time, but we stop here, on the boundary which divides ancient from modern entrancement, table-tipping and rapping.

CHAPTER VIII.

DEMONOLOGY, WITCHCRAFT, AND SPIRIT RAPPING, TIPPING, AND ENTRANCEMENT.

Old mythology has not removed the spirit-world very far from that of the real, even in what may be spoken of in the abstract as a measurable distance. Like the necropolis, where the dead slumber, and the weary are at rest, it is but as without the city walls, and in many a Mirza-vision the rapt and dreamy spiritualist of old would go forth in the cool of the evening, and, under the watching stars, by wild incantation cast the sombre pall aside, and gaze with an awful gladness into the mysteries of a life for which he was preparing himself by fast and vigils, by unbridled imagination, and by potent spell. Would not the "spirit" theory in ages of mysticism and symbol, when the sciences were accidents, and the half of the common, of a supernatural cast, strike the vulgar; would not its inventor impress the seal of his spirit on the age, and make his doctrine work anything he pleased in the way of conversion and of persuasion? Could he not lead the multitude as he pleased? What are the names of Zoroaster, of Pythagoras, of Plato, Zeno, Epicurus, and the rest, but indications of such teachings? Their immortality is the symbol of creeds that ruled thousands in their age, and ere, and long after. Could but the priestly lore of Egypt be deciphered now, we should see in the names of their theosophists those who formed her first creeds, and blended on one stock the stupendous in grace and grandeur, with the lowest and most debased forms of belief in the invisible, through symbol and through sign.

Crude at first, these ideas became polished, perfect agencies; a genealogy of gods once established, the qualities of life, motion, and matter, rendered impersonation necessary,—hence, gods, demigods, messengers, attributes, life in the air, earth, sea, and fire, life in the stem and the leaf, the grass, and descending dews. Poetry awoke and consecrated all with a tenderness, grace, and beauty, that recommended the system in various modes to all the human race.

Creating thus a future home, an Elysian garden, "a dwelling not made with hands," where the souls of heroes and good men were to dwell, and which the wicked, after long expiation, might attain, it was necessary that messengers, interpreters, and ministering angels should stand between man and Hades, and so expound to his tumultuous and thirsty mind what and who, and in what manner spirits dwell there. So arose the priest, the hierophant, the possessed, the magician, the wizard, sorcerer, and the long train of good and bad agencies, that have since filled the world with wonder and with awe.

It was not till after the advent of the Saviour that religion, grafted on paganism, took, with depraved and vulgar minds, those awful and harrowing depths of woe and despair which characterized the ages after the church was established. Tartarus and its fiery lakes surrendered to the penal Hell, to the "second death" of Irenæus, and to the expiatory pains of purgatory. Then, indeed, did the shadows of darkness fall on the moral world. The beautiful and benign system of atonement, as taught by the Scriptures, was hidden and encumbered by dread and terror. The gospel of love, preached but to a few, and not comprehended even by those, gave place to a gospel of terror, and to the dread anathemas of a church that sacrificed its divine kingdom to splendors and to dominancy over this. The haunted precincts of existence poured and vomited forth spectres and horrors, wraiths, demons, ghouls, and vampires. To play with the passions of the people was not difficult. Blue fires, subterranean, as also superterranean noises, ghastly midnight visitants, were easily worked. The little science that was known was enlisted by the crafty in this reign of terror, where they were potential, and panic became a moral chronic among men. For every thing that was grisly and appalling, the Witch of Endor served as a text. Sorcery had been forbidden by a king whose life was one long struggle with insane passions. Violent and haughty, he had disobeyed the commands of the Most High, and the hour of retribution was at hand. His Nemesis was stalking noiselessly behind him, out of sight, but she was already grasping at the royal fillet. To his palace gates rose the murmur of advancing foes: around him were cries of mutiny; and the horizon of his hopes grew dark, and dread, and hopeless, so that his bold soul shrank with a deadly and ominous fear. No longer came the warning dream, the voice of Urim in reply to prayer. The warnings of the prophets had been neglected, and, shrouded in gloom and despair, he sought the dwelling of the creature whose lips he had sealed with a sign, whose arts he had suspended by a word. In disguise he commands her to foretell to him his future. He is reminded of the king's edict, but in the tone of a king (which she could not mistake) he bids her fear nothing, and assures her of protection. The form and bearing of him who stood colossal in the tents of Israel might, if nothing else, have taught her who the visitant was. The hag begins; affects to behold spirits ascending, and is ordered to call up the spirit of Samuel. After cries of terror, she describes him as an old man enveloped in a mantle, which to Saul's excited imagination, became identical with Samuel. It was easy to predict the fate of one so beset and so crushed by misfortunes. Common rumor might tell the witch the few chances in his favor, the certain reverses gathering against him. In his great anguish and despair the monarch-soldier laments that God has forsaken him, and she confirms this despair by her sentence. Like a lion at bay she turns him in the battle. He beholds his army beaten, his sons slain, and, disdaining to be taken captive, falls on his own sword, and dies, as long after it was the "high Roman fashion" to die.

Sorcery, witchcraft, magic, divination, and the rest, became, on such authority as this, the great manias of the middle ages. What was grand in Greek and other antique mythology became hideous here. Nemesis pursuing crime; the Eumenides lashing with remorse and terror the wicked and the doomed, the fatal sisters presiding over birth, and destiny, and death, have something grand about them, something suggestive in their separate spheres of action: but in the witch sabbaths, and demon revels, ghostly hauntings, and other churchyard horrors of succeeding ages, nothing but the lowest elements of the horrible are perceptible.

In reading of these delusions of the past, by which the structure of society was shaken to its basis, civilization retarded and otherwise fatally injured, and the whole business of life paralyzed, we cannot help being struck with the occasional developments of insanity that occurred on such scales of magnitude, and so repeatedly. Free as we are from any such tendencies at the present day—though spirit manifestations did indeed threaten a revolution of the popular mind,—it seems one of the marvels of the impossible, that thousands of persons—no rank, no condition, no age or sex, excepted—should seize a belief, a mania like the plague, and act and argue, as if they were in the literal bonds of the Evil One. The stories told would be all very well as the ingenious exercises of a fantastic mind, but these traditions of *diablerie* handed down, are incontrovertible truths, and cannot but impress us with a pity for the imbecility of human intellect at different stages, whatever we may say of its powers in other respects.

Periodical insanity on a gigantic scale there undoubtedly was, and wisdom and eld left aside duty and labor to follow the hysterical troop that, dancing, and sometimes naked, went like frantic Corybantes through the streets of European capitals. In hysterical catalepsy, they were borne off to wizard heights,

> " With birch and with broom,
> Over stick, over stone ;"

where Pandemonium had sent a deputation to meet them, and where they held their dreadful orgies. This was the active development of those delusions. Melancholy madness, dementia, asceticism, fanaticism, the scourge, fasting, exacerbation, and the rest, completed it, and exhibited its passive phase. We have nothing that *we* know of, in the shape of treatise or discourse written at those periods, that serves to cast a judicial or clinical light on the matter. A verbose record of the events is all, and these are many, for the manias are many. Their name was legion. In one instance thousands of children went wandering through the country, and died in groups. In another, crowds of men went lashing and scourging themselves through the public streets. These anarchies were composed of indecency, obscenity, blasphemy, and disease, such as we have no other parallels on record for ; unless, indeed, the Scriptures may supply us with circumstances approximating

—the worshipping of Moloch, leprosy, demoniacal possession, and so forth.

One reason why such a mania, when it occurred, grew apace so rapidly, and infected such numbers, was, doubtless, the ignorance that existed as regarded mental pathology, and the consequent lack of asylums and mad-houses, where the mischief might have been checked ere it grew to a head. There was no want of room. Convent and cloister, monastery and cathedral appendages, would have suffered for the temporary hospital. There was no want of men and women good and zealous, as human nature has ever shown in times of great requirement, but there was a total lack of the physician to watch the diagnostics of the disease. There was a lack, perhaps, in the therapeutics of the day, though few drugs or mandragora would have been required. The frenzy had its way. Time and intelligence alone could cure it. The lazar-houses held their share, the barren wastes theirs. The tomb covers all now, and only the memory (a sad and mournful one enough) remains to mark the events that passed by like a convulsion, and carried its victims off with it.

The apparition and the phantom were other crude deposits of these monstrous things. We have something like a knowledge that only a thin tenebrous veil lies between us and that solemn land, where each spectre takes its solitary way to grief or glory. But this veil, like that of Isis, has never been lifted up. At times—for we cannot deny nor assert the possibility—at times, we repeat, dusky visages, shadows of shapes, glaring forms, may come to the other side of the veil, and so far make themselves palpable to us—so far even as to touch with a breath—to startle with a sigh, to condense that essence to the sense of touch, or to what is to the imagination its equivalent; and thus to give us all the impress and all the awe of a communion near or distant with the spirits of those who dwell beyond 'the portal,' where we should have thought no cares, instincts, and ties of this life would have entered, but have been left behind, like the Christian's burden, at the foot of the Cross.

Palingenesey, or the reproduction of the original to infinity, from its ashes, if not the real groundwork of the theory of apparitions, at least gave it consecutiveness, force, and the direct influence of collateral evidence. One portion of these theories, too, was to insist upon a kind of material soul, which, by some inherent attraction, still lingered in the mundane sphere, and, by the force of an attraction which is a part of the mysterious whole, was still drawn towards those it loved and dwelt with upon earth; and, if nothing more, gave signs of its existence, its anxiety and interest in their welfare.

Lavater, at a later time, and with him Mesmer, so we take it, gave to the strength of the imagination a controlling magnetic force, by which it was capable, at any distance, of impressing and influencing the like emotions in other individuals. This idea has been expanded by the founder of the Odylic theory, until it has become one of the logical weapons in the hands of the magnetist, and manifestor, or medium. On the other hand, science has treated apparitions with a lofty sort of scorn, and, by creating for itself an hypothesis, has talked learnedly of latent impression, of optical delusion, of the retina of reflection, refraction—what not? In this respect, however, science has done good service. It has prevented us from rushing into delusion headlong. Has it done a corresponding evil, that of making men rush into the extreme of doubt and skepticism? We doubt.

Lenses, concave mirrors, the forming of phantoms in the air by some *simulacra* cast from a reflecting body, might do much to move wonder and excite the mind. The repetition of these weakened the results; for they required a kind of animation, and the figures of colossal gods ever so grand and august, if they move not, speak not, thunder not, become like the productions of the chisel, mighty and supernal sculptures, awakening admiration at their beauty and proportion. The supernatural dies away.

But fiery lights, corruscations, figures in motion, revive what was decaying. The conjuror must learn more to be perfect. Yet more revelations of the spirit-land must be granted, ere man will totally be subjected. The fable of the Dioscuri is one that we cannot but admire for its several striking graces; but if we attempt to account for their appearance in the capitol, or at the great battle, striking and strident, by the theory of optical delusion, practised by some sage *flamen*, all that we have gained in the impress of the sublime and the awful, perishes under the arid mathematics of light and shadow, and we are once more of the earth—earthy. On the contrary, if the spiritual vision cannot be argued away, what an increase is there to the faith that only wanted the slightest confirmation to carry its belief to any extent!

To reduce this to theory—to bring it within the bounds of probability—let us imagine the following:

A son mourning for a beloved parent—or a husband sorrowing in a sobbing anguish for the wife of his bosom—or a father, in love and awe, in the unspeaking pains of separation from that bud of promise, that apple of the eye which is now growing in the garden of God, shall in lonely meditation dwell upon that face and form, which now no more, were dearer to him than all the world beside.

Surrounded by the silence of his room, while the cool twilight of a summer bathes his brow, he gazes abstractedly through the opened window at the coming stars flooding the azure floor of heaven; pressed by thick coming fancies, he surrenders himself to those memories so dear—hears one by one the tones wake, the sweet voice flow, the oral music loosed—sees (in fancy) hair wave, eyes flash, and smiles dimpling the cheek. The parent is lost in dream-land, seeking for his child beloved, and with a consciousness that it is near him, but that he is also nearer to earth, he casts himself with all the force of a will becoming entranced, into the search his soul is now, with every effort, making. And dear remembrances, tiny embraces, fond caresses, such as pass between child and parent, come with a redoubled reality to him. The scene changes: light is broader. The sun shines on that fair forehead: the child is at play; it laughs, it touches his knees!

What, all at once, makes the man start, turn pale, gaze with all his soul into space, and experience an awe, half terror, half love, as the nerves thrill and the hair creeps? Tears are in his eyes, palpitation is at his heart, and the *globus hystericus* well nigh chokes him. He has *seen his dead darling!* He has heard that soft, soft voice again. The tiny hand has touched him!

Such may be the *rationale* of a spirit visit, which taking other coincidences of time into consideration, no argument, or any usual means of conviction adopted, will ever persuade me to the contrary. The paradox is too, that the same individual may reject the ghost-theory in the main, and this proves not only the whole difficulty of ever adjusting the matter while in uncertainty he wavers between two opinions. It is only necessary that the medium, with his "manifestations," should step in, and make of him a conquest to his faith for ever.

During partial darkness, the eye assumes certain impressionable conditions. In order to pierce the gloom, and to collect whatever amount of feeble light there is, the pupil undergoes an expansion to the whole width of the iris, and it is shown that in this state the pupil fails to accommodate itself to the clear perception of any object at hand; consequently, shapes and forms at a distance, become vague and confused; at that distance, we calculate, we can best behold them. In this state, the eye is favorable to the production of any kind of optical delusion, and in this state too, the imagination is most easily excited. Now, these spectral forms assume a white or greyish hue, as no actual color can be decidedly pronounced upon, and those objects which most reflect the little amount of corpuscular rays in the chamber, or which may be projected from a luminous ground, or by anything animate that may actually, or by reflection, pass across the surface of this ground, also assume that spectral aspect which it is the province of the illusion to produce. The eye, strained to the utmost, discerning an inanimate object whose different projections reflect light in different degrees, is enabled to obtain a more sustained and collected view; but a constant evanescence, and a constant recurrence also take place, and the necessary change of outline following hard on this, will give it the semblance of a living or moving form. Meanwhile, it depends upon the coolness and courage of the spectator to advance and dispel the illusion, or, seized with a nameless fear, to transform it into an apparition, and invest it with the features of the well-known form of some one, living or dead, who dwells most dominant in the spectator's mind. This eluding and again consubstantiating form or shape, traced in such a twilight, would take such a gliding motion as is usually attributed to ghosts; and though there may be no actual movement from the spot, there is so much that is like it, as to render the delusive phantasy perfect.

Thus, then, those inclined to superstition, or who are under the influence of dread, receive such confirmation of their fears, as to create grounds for an authenticated ghost-story; and add to this the known integrity of the narrator, when he gives his assurance that such a visitation or manifestation has been made him, that he must be skeptical indeed who will not go far to give implicit credence to the wildest and most wondrous tale.

The apparitions of Nicolai, the German bookseller, are too familiar to need more than a reference to, being illustrations of the case in point, and evidently the result of optical delusion, arising from the disordered state of the nervous system, and a consequent derangement in the faculty of sight. Other very singular examples too, may be found in Sir David Brewster's work on "Natural Magic."

Those who would argue the probabilities of a writing-medium from some such event as the hand-writing on Belshazzar's palace walls, and point out to the unknown nature of the characters as a coincidence carrying proof, do not hesitate to prove "possession," and from the authority given in the narrative respecting the demons of the Gadarene swine. But such persons argue on grounds that assume more than we grant to them, for the plain reason that all relative conditions between man and his Maker are so far changed as to render such manifestations unnecessary and unmeaning. The writing on the wall, and the possessed by Legion, the demons and the swine, were all necessary, and had a meaning, neither of which it is our place or inclination to explain or reason upon.

CHAPTER IX.

COMMENTS ON THE AUTHOR'S VISITS AMONG THE RAPPERS.

So far, in this, our second book of the "Rappers," we have given principally the theories and reflections of others, in explanation of these phenomena which we are contemplating. We have pursued this course, because we wished to place the whole subject completely before the reader, in all the light of elucidation which has been thrown upon it from any source. We shall now proceed to speak wholly for ourself.

In the two preceding chapters we have traced the ancient history of "Rapping," and run briefly over the whole ground of ancient demonology, entrancement, and witchcraft. We have done this simply because we consider "modern spiritualism," as it is called, but a grand sublimation, and reducing into something like form, all the phenomena of ancient oracles, raps, tips, demonology, divine ecstacy, &c. All the instances of ancient rapping, tipping, &c., which we have cited are those wherein no trick is discoverable, or at least proved, and have remained, since their occurrence, misty and indefinite, with nothing on their face but the allegation that they were intelligences from another world. These ancient rappings, which have been paralleled by modern ones, have been taken up by the enterprise and ingenuity of the nineteenth century, and made to come out of the mist of indefiniteness, have had a form and a language given to them, and a religion, or, rather, a theory of miscalled religion, built upon them. It was a low and vulgar form of alleged spiritual agency to render definite, and on which to build another temple of faith to supersede that temple of Jesus Christ, in which no tables tip and no raps are heard, in order to open a communication between spirits and mortals. But modern spiritualists have chosen these low alleged spirit rappings for their superstructure, and by them they must be judged. To the United States belongs the credit, if credit it is, of first reducing into form ancient rappings, giving them a regular language, with all the adjuncts of reading, writing, and arithmetic, and building on them, as we said before, a new religious structure.

The first case of a "rapping" nature, of any great notoriety, which we hear of in the United States, occurred at Penobscot, Maine, and a Mr. Dods, (not the author whom we have before mentioned in this volume, but a merchant of the above town) was the "medium." The first intimations which Mr. Dods received of the honor intended for him, were conveyed by rappings in the wall, now here, now there—evidently not one second in the same spot. Although he—especially at first—deemed these noises very strange and very mysterious, their frequency deprived them of their greatest terror, and gradually reconciled the Dods' family to their determined continuance. Perhaps displeased at the growing indifference which the Dods displayed towards the "rappings," the unseen agency was driven to exhibit the presence of greater power. At all events, Mr. Dods had reason to think so. One evening, after having transacted some mercantile affairs in town, he was returning home "as sober as a judge," when he beheld the school-room which was near his home brilliantly illuminated, and, to all appearance, the scene of great festivity. Amazed that any proceedings, on so grand a scale as the aspect of the school-room denoted, could have been contemplated, much less going on, without his knowledge, he hastened to the spot, and all became suddenly dark—the stars quietly shining overhead—the school-house a gloomy spectacle, not enlivened by a solitary light. Under the natural impression that such a change could not have been so perfectly accomplished in so short a time, he rubbed his eyes to ascertain if anything had interfered with his vision, but nothing satisfied the search. He next ran to the door, thinking that the scholars, if they had, as was by no means usual, collected for a jollification, might have been induced to extinguish the lights upon hearing that he approached. The opening of the school-door, and standing in the midst of the room, was the work of an instant, but a work which increased the wonder of Dods, as nothing was visible but empty benches, barely seen, and not a stir was heard. This was a variation in the manifestations for which the family were unprepared, and the mere rappings dwindled to nothing in its presence. But the rapping was also susceptible of a variation, and soon declared itself like a heavy metal ball rolling along the attic, and reverberating through the whole house. Not content with this change, a new phase was adopted, in the turning of tables, stirring of beds, running hither and thither of lights, and endless other similar singular demonstrations. The scene of these phenomena was visited by so many persons, that the Clerk of the County Courts, with his assistants, deemed it his duty to attend at the spot, and endeavor to detect and expose the trick, if a trick were detectable. Mr. Dods permitted them to select their own apartment, where they were left in quiet possession about 9 o'clock in the evening. Having taken every necessary precaution, and seen that it was impossible for any human being to be concealed in the chamber, or able to obtain admission without their knowledge; having also narrowly examined the entire apartment, and found it free from all machinery,—they retired, without having extinguished the candle. Soon afterwards, bed and bed-clothes grew so unmanageable, and went through so many strange freaks, that these men, without obtaining the slightest clue to the mystery, gave up the adventure and its object as hopeless. It was said, that in the absence of Mr. Dods the manifestations did not occur.

Many cases of the like sort occurred in various parts, creating considerable excitement, but it was not until the year 1848, that they reached their culminating point. At this time certain mysterious noises were heard in the family of John D. Fox, at Rochester, New York, and the fame thereof soon spread through the country. Crowds flocked to the residence of the Foxes, and the knockings increased in frequency and force inside the house, while wonder and speculation increased in the same proportion, both far and near, outside the humble dwelling, which became a kind of knocking Mecca to which the eyes and steps of all the pilgrims of curiosity instinctively were turned. But this time, the raps were not suffered to die away and dissolve into air, without an attempt, at least, to nail them. By a long series of experiments, the raps meaning "yes," and the raps meaning "no," and the raps meaning "I don't know," "perhaps so," "may be so," and "may be not," "doubtful," "partly so," and "partly not," were discovered, or rather figured out, by the Foxes, and the spirits now began to talk with the Foxes quite glibly, as far as monosyllables went. But discovery did not end here. Yankee ingenuity brought forth an alphabetical card, and the Foxes soon had an interesting school of spirits, in which they taught the spirits their letters. The spirits learned rapidly and could soon spell out whole sentences, for the edification of their mortal hearers. Arithmetic was taught them by card in the same manner, and soon the spirits, if a mortal pointed to a figure on the card, knew it in a moment, and rapped loudly their knowledge thereof. From the alphabet and the arithmetical card, the spirits made suddenly a tremendous jump in their education, and seizing hold of the arms and hands of their favorites, galvanized them into a species of writing, which, to judge by its eccentric lines and curves, might have been produced by the powers of another world, for no mortal keenness of perception, although as sinuous and twisting as that said to be possessed by mortal lawyers, could read it and give the interpretation thereof. But the same power which galvanized the hands of the mediums into writing, seemed also to galvanize them into perception, and no sooner was the writing produced than the mediums read it as plain as print. And thus the spiritual mediums write and read at the present moment, with perhaps a little improvement on the commencement.

But the spirits, or rather the "rappers," did not stop at reading, writing, and arithmetic. As, after the Fox development at Rochester, knockings and raps and tipping tables became frequent all over the country, there was added another phase of progress in this so called spiritual phenomena. The spirits began to speak through mediums, dance through the mediums, and roll and tumble about through the mediums. In other words, the so called spirits "took possession" of the mediums, spoke through them, and performed all manner of antics through them. And at this point of spiritual rapping history, the phenomena of ancient demonology, witchcraft, and entrancement, joins, and becomes blended with, the phenomena of ancient rappings and table tipping. And thus blended, in our opinion, they stand now, and stood when we made our visit among the "Rappers," the particulars of which are recorded in the first part of this volume.

Looking back on our visits among the "Spirit Circles" as they are called, and asking our readers also to take the same retrospective glance in the faithful description we have given of the scenes witnessed by us, we are struck, at the first start, and we think our readers will likewise be struck in the same manner, with the incongruity of rapping, tapping, and entranced manifestations, with the idea that these manifestations emanate from spirits. Did we actually, we said to ourself, come in contact with a spirit? were we in actual communication with the departed of earth, disrobed of their gross corporeal forms, and standing around us, shadowy and invisible, but still whole and perfect forms of spiritual existence, talking to us or others near us, making themselves manifest and uniting palpably, as it were, the land of spirits with the land of mortals? If it were so, it was a grand and awful circle for us or any other mortal to be in. If it were so, would not some invisible power of awe, and grandeur, and reverence, have chained the soul of every one present? Would not the atmosphere, if we may so express ourself, of the land of spirits, have filled the room, and every head been bent in involuntary attention? We think so. But our head was not bent, —our soul was chained by no invisible power,—we felt no atmosphere of spirit land. Gladly would we have breathed such an atmosphere,—gladly would we have had our soul enchained by such a power,—joyfully would we have bowed our head to listen to those whom we had loved on earth. We were passive,—open to the slightest impression, but the atmosphere of the spirit land was not there,—there was no spirit power or chain to bend our head or bind our soul either in respect, in awe, or fear. It is easy for a believer in rapping manifestations to say, that we were not in a state to be impressed, that we were too "positive," that we were an unbeliever, or even a scoffer, but this, in opinion, amounts to nothing; if we had been in actual communication with spirits,—if spirits had actually come to earth to talk to us, manifest themselves to us, and were actually in the room with us for that purpose, we should have been *made* to feel, else why did they enact the farce of coming? No, we did not feel,—there was no spirit power or chain upon us from the fact of the incongruity of the manner of the manifestation with the idea of spirits. So far from either respect or awe, or fear being upon us, our mind involuntarily, as we sat at the table and heard the sounds thereon, reverted back to the negro melody which we had often heard at Woods' and Christy's Minstrels, the most remarkable line of which is—

"Who's dat knockin' at de door."

And in this reversion of our thoughts we could not help coming to the conclusion that there was as much of the appearance of the influence of spirits about the stage of Woods' and Christy's Minstrel Hall as about the table of the "Spirit Circle," in which we were sitting.

It cannot be! this very low, vulgar, ludicrous, and at times, revolting manner of the alleged spirit manifestations, by means of knocks, rapping-tables, and contorting the bodies of the Mediums, proves, at the very start, a fatal objection to, and repels the mind against, the idea that spiritual intelligences have any connection with the matter.

"But," perhaps, says the reader, "is it not strange that when a number of names of living and dead persons are written on slips of paper, carefully folded up and placed upon the table by the questioner, who alone knows what the names are, is it not strange that the table will tip or rap at the right one?"

It is very strange at first sight, we admit, but experience among "Spirit Circles," such as we have had, will prove that in this matter of picking out names, the wrong ones are about as often designated by the raps or tips, as the right ones, which fact robs the phenomenon of some of its strangeness, and throws about it an air of chance which does not speak much, to say the least of it, for spiritual knowledge. The same remark applies to the telling of ages, places of death, diseases, &c., as designated by raps or tips when the questioner writes them down on a slip of paper, and points with his pencil as we have described in the first book of this volume.

"But" again, says the reader, "is there not something mysterious in the many communications written by Mediums, in the speeches made by them when in a state of entrancement, and do not these writings and speeches exhibit an intelligence outside of and beyond the Mediums themselves?"

In a few instances, we admit we have seen communications written by Mediums, and heard speeches delivered by them, which were characterized by a mystery which we cannot pretend wholly to fathom; but in the majority of the written communications and the speeches which we have read and heard, there was nothing but what any mortal might write or speak—the general character of all communications and speeches professing to come from spirits, are, as far as our experience goes, either common letters of affection, and addressed generally "dear mother," "dear daughter," or "dear father," &c., as the case may be, but with no names either of addresser or addressed, especially when the communication is a first one; or else they are rhapsodies, written and spoken and characterized by a collection of fine words, and nothing but words, about the beauty of the spirit land, the future triumph of spirtualism, and rejoicings that the subject is awakening so much attention. As to conveying any tangible information of practical benefit, or giving tests that the spirits speaking or writing are the spirits of those they represent themselves to be, our experience has been that such information or such tests are rarely given; on the contrary the so called spirits are positively ugly on this point. They will write whole sheets of foolscap, and talk by the hour on all sorts of subjects where words only are needed, but ask them to write or speak *one word*, which will convey a test of their identity, and they are silent. The proof of the above remarks will be found in a careful examination of our tour among the "Rappers."

"But," again says the reader, "can you explain that scene of exorcism in your visit among the "Rappers," in which it is represented that an evil spirit is cast out of the young girl Medium?"

The scene certainly looks very startling on its face, but we think the explanation is easy. The girl Medium was simply in a pscychological state, and the mind of him, at whose command she returned to her natural state, was stronger than hers, and according to rules of pscychological science, produced therefore the effect which we witnessed and have described.

There is another point on which we have to remark, in connection with our experience among the Rappers, and that is, that we have often noticed in our own visits, particularly among the public Mediums, that the Mediums had power to stop the raps or tips at their will. We have noticed more than once, that when the time devoted to sittings was up, or when a Medium did not appear to be in a very good humor, or seemed in a hurry to have the visitors leave, the raps suddenly stopped, and there was spelt out, or written out, "good night," or "good bye," or "good morning," &c., as the case might be. There was no use of trying to get manifestations, after such latter manifestoes from the spirits as the above. We do not mean by this to charge trick on the part of the Mediums, for we believe that the raps and tips which we heard and saw in the presence of the Mediums referred to, were not produced by any trick; but we mean only to say that the raps and tips are under the control of the Medium, which proves to our mind conclusively, that the raps and tips are something emanating from, and are a part and parcel of, the Mediums, how or in what manner they may not know themselves, but still such an inherent, although mysterious power, belonging to them, and which they control, as proves that the raps and tips belong to them alone, and spirits have nothing to do with the production. We think, in fact, that this power of the Mediums to control the noises and the tables, although there is no trick in the matter, one of the most convincing proofs of the absence of all spiritual influence. And the Mediums can also control their hands and entrancements in the same manner. At least, so we think, from all we have seen, and we have looked pretty sharply. If they resist the influence that is seizing their hand to write, or twisting their eyes and bodies into a trance, we have often noticed that neither trance or writing came. And we have again noticed them gliding into both with all the ease possible, as if they wished to do so, and knew they would not be disappointed.

Another singular development in this rapping phenomena strikes us as we look back on our visits among the "Spirit Circles." If the reader will peruse carefully our account, he will find in the communications of the alleged spirits, such a collection of contradictions and direct foolish lies, as any sane mortal would be ashamed to utter. If they are spirits who utter these contradictions and lies, then demonology and witchcraft are true to the letter, and these spirits called up by modern Rappers are devils. But we do not believe that spirits of any kind are connected with this phenomena. We believe the whole mystery is in the still unexplained mysteries of magnetism, electricity, clairvoyance and pschycology, or rather in the mysterious mixture, if we may so express ourself, of the whole of these.

It is not to be doubted but that animal magnetism (and, as a matter of course, most of its modern adjuncts) has been familiar to the world under other names, and in the forms of demonology, witch-mania, and the rest.

This mesmeric phenomenon renders the patient insensible to pain. It is in fact antalgic; but, in return, it asserts mastery over the human individual will. The clairvoyant has a capacity for speaking languages the person has never known—for observing organic diseases in others—for seeing beyond the limits of vision—for the faculty of sharing in some way the thoughts of others, or of anticipating them—for resisting the action of fire, for a period at least—for being in effect the agent that acts between the immaterial and the material worlds. The clairvoyant cannot explain the theory, or give a lucid reason for such. The operator is as little able, except by conjecture, comparison, and the like.

This condition may be produced spontaneously. By fixing the eye upon an object, by concentrating the thought upon an idea, by isolating one's self in the completest manner from all surrounding and extraneous things, the state of semi-trance may be induced. It is thus that a concentration of the magnetic fluid is gathered or absorbed, and the results are in like proportion. A writer plausibly asserts that this must have been the foundation of the epidemic manias, and that the contagion multiplied in its intensity of communication, as the numbers increased, and the magnetic electricity became centered among them.

We cannot but agree with those who refer to electricity as the generator and true motive-power of the whole phenomena, witnessed and detailed; though the manifestations that are produced are in so many ways dissimilar to all known developments of that fluid. "This interior concussion of particles," says an intelligent examiner of the system, "which occurs in the ordinary sounds (rapping, &c.,) can be attributed to no other cause than the permeation and action of some subtle essence analogous to electricity. It is, accordingly, another important fact, that persons of delicate nerves can generally feel abundant evidence of the action of such an essence, while the phenomena in question are occurring.

That the system is capable of gathering within it, and of giving out by contact, or by distant affinity, currents of the electric fluid, is now a matter, we think, beyond question. This is termed vital electricity, and of a kind that is not evolved in the common and usual developments of that agent. It is controllable by the mind of another as often as it may be; and certainly more so under the control of the person himself, especially if, in addition to a susceptible organization, the strength of will is more than usually marked. In this case, however, a "reflex current is also continuously running back to the brain, to convey to it the consciousness of the act with the hand. In the case of the so-called spirit-meetings, although the act may have originated in the individual's own brain, and a current passed to the hand, dictating the performance of certain acts or motions, yet no current returns to convey an idea of the performance of such acts by the hand. The current may be supposed to pass off from the person;" and, reasoning from this, it may be assumed that this "detached vital electricity" may operate much in like manner on the system of another.

It is, therefore, this vital electricity, this odylic fluid, that should now occupy the attention of the learned, of the earnest, of the seeker after truth, unless we are content to stop short at the advent of a strange and unaccountable agent, and leave it to take its course; the foolish to be deluded, the credulous to believe anything, and the indifferent to see a perilous matter growing to a head. By diligent observation and inquiry something more that we yet lack must ultimately be found out; that something may lead us to the final principle which now eludes us. To the solution of this many years to come must be dedicated. And in future years, we doubt not, that the whole of the "Rappers" will be clearly explained on such scientific principles as will sweep away all ideas of spiritual agency in the matter. What science now reveals on this subject, only in part, will be opened in full; although the world may continue full of "rappings" of various kinds, *spirit* rappings will be no more.

CHAPTER X.

THE RELIGION OF JESUS CHRIST AND THE RELIGION OF RAPPERS.

THE religion, of which Jesus Christ was the great founder and teacher, is simple and sublime. It is not our province, neither is it our purpose, to enter into argumentative details of this religion, or give the various phases of doctrine which it assumes among the many different sects of its disciples. We design rather to exhibit it briefly in its principal features, and by way of contrast to another religion which has been developed in the nineteenth century,—we design simply to place, side by side, the religion of Christ and the religion of Rappers.

The text book of the religion of Jesus Christ is the Bible. It is claimed by Christians, that this Bible is the inspired word of God to man, spoken by God himself to prophets, and by them recorded,—spoken by the Son of God himself, while living on earth as a man, to his apostles, and by them also written down. It matters not, as far as it regards the view we are now taking, that this claim for the foundation of the Christian religion has been disputed by many in all ages of the world. Disputed or undisputed, one fact stands out bold and incontrovertible--no sophistry can sweep it away, and no denunciation can lessen its force. That fact is, that the origin claimed for the Christian religion, and the foundation on which it is made to rest, are in themselves sublime—just such an origin and a foundation as a religion, by which man is to live and die, should have—the direct word of God to man, written, it is true, by mortals, but dictated to the writers by God himself,—a sacred charter of faith, delivered to man by no secondary spirit from a lower sphere of the spirit world, but dictated to man, and signed, sealed, and delivered to man, by God himself, sitting on his throne in the highest of the heavens. So much for the origin of the Religion of Christ as claimed by its believers.

The religion of Jesus Christ teaches than man is twofold—mortal and immortal—mortality for this world, and immortality for the world of spirits. It believes, that when the body dies, it returns to dust, while the soul passes into another world—the souls of the believing and the righteous into a world of bliss, and the souls of the unbelieving and wicked into a world of misery. It teaches that when the designs of God shall be accomplished in regard to the human race, that then there shall come a day of general resurrection, when the bodies of all men shall rise from their graves and be united to their souls—and that then body and soul united, all men shall stand before God in general judgment--the believers and the righteous to be received into Heaven, and the unbelieving and the wicked to be turned into Hell. A particular and literal description of the place of departed spirits, between the death of the body and the general resurrection, and of the Heaven and the Hell which follows the general judgment, is not given in the Bible—the only description that the Bible gives is figurative language, expressing the greatest misery and the highest happiness. And it is not necessary for us here to enter into any of the many speculations which have been broached on the subject of the particular nature of the place of departed spirits, and of the Heaven and Hell, set forth in the Bible—the great doctrine is one of future rewards and punishment, and this is all with which we have now to do, in giving this brief synopsis of the religion of Christ.

And this religion of Jesus Christ has also a spirit doctrine, the most sublime and holy in its nature. It teaches that a Holy Spirit, not an indefinite impulse or essence of good, but a real Spirit, equal with the Father and the Son, is ever around and in man to impel him forward to good, and deter and save him from evil—even the spirit of the Holy Ghost. It teaches that man's soul and body are the temple of the Holy Ghost, and that the Holy Ghost will not leave that temple, unless driven from it by man himself, through acts of wickedness and sin. Thus, according to the doctrine of the Christian religion, God himself, in the presence of the Holy Ghost, is a spirit ever dwelling in man, talking to him and communicating with him; it is no secondary spirit, but the spirit of God himself, which manifests itself to man in man, and man can at any time call that spirit up and hold communion with it. Can any spirit doctrine be more sublime than this? Again, it is an old belief among, we believe, almost every sect of Christians, that the Bible, although it does not directly teach, leaves the reader to draw a fair inference, that all men have continually about them a guardian spirit, an invisible but still real personal spirit, not of a departed mortal friend, but a pure immortal spirit of Heaven, guarding and watching over them, and ever striving on one side of man to counteract the influence of an evil spirit—the devil, which is ever walking on the other side.

This religion of Jesus Christ stops not here in the mere promulgation of certain doctrines for belief. It erects a form of government for Christians in their religious belief, binds them together in a church, with Christ for its head, and laws and ordinances for its governance, and thus makes that religion one of order and combined practical effect.

Centuries on centuries have rolled on, and this religion of Christ has prevailed over a large part of the world. Its practical working has been of such a nature as to elevate the human race higher, and make them better than any other form of religion has ever yet done. It has been at once a restraint from evil and an incentive to good, and millions have died attesting its truth with their dying breath. Shall it be swept away? shall it be injured in the slightest degree, in its integrity, by a new religion? Not unless the new religion is better and can produce higher claims for belief than the old. The religion of the "Rappers" proposes to sweep it away, for it discards it and seeks to introduce a substitute. What is that substitute? Let us see.

The religion of the Rappers has no text-book, has no Bible, no charter, and it claims none. But does it not claim an origin, a foundation, from which it springs? Yes, and the origin and the foundation are, raps produced by invisible agency on tables, walls, &c., tables tipping up in all manner of ludicrous ways, speeches through entrancement, and writings through the involuntary movement of the hand. And what produces the raps, the tips, the speeches of entrancement and the writing? Do the Rappers claim that God, through the raps and tips, the entrancement and the writing, speaks to man? No. Do they claim, that spirits from around the throne of God, and sent by God, speak to man in this singular manner? No. In the religion of the Rappers, the sublime doctrine of God speaking to man, is cast aside—as far as we have learned the doctrine of the Rappers, God has nothing to do with the manifestations. The Rappers say, that the raps, the tips, the entrancement, and the writing, so far from being produced by God, or spirits which have never been mortal, are produced only by the spirits of those who have once been mortal, but who have departed this life, or "left the form," as they say—that some of these spirits are good, some undeveloped or rather half bad, but progressing to be better, and that all of them, through the language of raps and tips, as reduced to an alphabet by mortals, and though speeches of entrancement and written communications speak to man, sometimes the truth, sometimes lies, sometimes in contradiction of themselves, often in a jocular and humbugging way, often in a mystified manner, and sometimes in a strain of sublimity—a strange mixture of material rapping, turning over of tables, ringing of bells, rhapsodies of speech, and galvanic writing. And yet such is the origin of, such the foundation on which rests that religion of "Rappers," which seeks to invalidate the religion of Jesus Christ. As it regards the origin and foundation claimed by both religions, we can only say—look on this picture and look on that—the Bible direct from God himself on the one hand—knocks, dancing tables, and misty entrancements on the other.

The religion of the Rappers teaches nothing more nor less than practical materialism. The scriptures are set aside with the most sublime indifference—there is no heaven, no hell, no future reward or punishment—all restraint from acting just as they choose, while here on earth, is taken, by this religion, from mortals—sin at pleasure, for the mortal man here is but an immaturity of development which shall become perfect in the spirit land. The religion of Rappers is thus an apologist for sin. If a man has been good on earth, it is all the better for him when he dies and enters the fanciful collection of spheres into which the Rappers divide the spirit world. If he has been a bad man on earth, why then it will not be quite so well for him at last; but it will not be very bad, and the progression in the spheres will eventually make it extremely good. On this accommodating system of the sphere, hinges all the religion of the Rappers. The following description of the spheres is in the words of the Rappers themselves:

"Commencing at the earth's centre, and proceeding outward in all directions, the surrounding space is divided into seven concentric spheres, rising one above and outside the other. Each of these seven 'spheres' or spaces is again divided into seven equal parts, called 'circles,' so that the whole 'spirit-world' consists of an immense globe of ether divided into seven spheres, and forty-nine circles, and in the midst of which our own globe is located. * * * The good, bad, and indifferent qualities of the spirits located in these seven separate spheres are carefully classified. * * * Those of the first sphere are said to be endowed with wisdom, wholly selfish, or seeking selfish good. 2nd. Wisdom controlled by popular opinion. 3rd. Wisdom independent of popularity, but not perfected. 4th. Wisdom which seeks others' good, and not evil. 5th. Wisdom in purity. 6th. Wisdom in perfection, to prophesy. 7th. Wisdom to instruct all others of less wisdom. According to the new philosophy, when a man dies, his soul ascends at once to that sphere for which it is fitted by knowledge and goodness on earth; and from that point ascends or progresses outward from circle to circle, and from sphere to sphere, increasing in knowledge and happiness as it goes, till it reaches the seventh circle of the seventh sphere, which is the highest degree of knowledge and bliss to which it is possible to attain in the spirit-world. They assert that heaven is beyond all the spheres, and represent the change from the seventh sphere to heaven, as equivalent to the change from the life on earth to a dwelling in the lower spheres. They are ever advancing and growing better. They can descend through all the intervening spheres to the rudimental, and help their tardy brethren *up;* yet their lower or vulgar spirits can never pull their more advanced brethren down."

The Rapping religion also speaks of a high degree of social affability existing among the dwellers of the zones—music, dancing, together with very praiseworthy efforts in the educational rudiments of reading, writing, and the like. There is "no marrying, or given in marriage," among them, but every spirit "has its partner of the opposite sex." They have seldom been united upon earth, a fact that implies a love of harmony, and a distaste to recommence any past connubial bickering that may have existed. These partners, however, have, for the most part, known each other, been intimates, friends, &c. We are also told by this religion of the rappers, that the spirits "have the power of creating whatever they desire. Whatever robes they desire to wear, they possess with the wish. They paint, sculpture, write, or compose music, and their productions are as tangible to them, as ours to us. The artist by means of his will, paints a picture, and shows it to his friends, as really as it is on earth; and the poet writes, and finds admirers of his verses, as he would here. They enjoy whatever they desire, and this is one of the sources of their happiness. They eat fruit, or whatever they incline to, and indulge their appetites—

not however, from necessity; they never feel hunger or thirst, or cold or heat. * * * If they wish for a harp, they at once possess it, and it is a reality—a tangible thing, and, to their perception, as much a material substance as the things we handle here.

The Rappers have no church, no reducing into governmental form their religion, no ordinances, no exercises of religion to elevate man from earth to heaven. The Rapper has no prayer; at least this is the legitimate tendency of the religion taught by Rappers. The legs of a table and entrancements and spirit-writings are both the Rapper's church and his religious services, his priest, and his ordinances. As for prayer, why should he pray?

We have done. We consider the religion of the Rappers to be blasphemy, and all its manifestations delusions. What its tendency must be, when thus it throws off all restraint from man, can easily be seen. Whether it is worthy either in sublimity, in appearance of truth, or in the least element of practical good, to supersede the religion of Jesus Christ, we leave the reader to judge for himself, from the picture of contrast which we have drawn.

FINIS.

THE LAWYER'S STORY,

OR,

THE ORPHAN'S WRONGS.

BY A MEMBER OF THE NEW-YORK BAR.

Beautifully Illustrated.

☞ The publishers have great pleasure in introducing this work to the public. As a family novel it is unexceptionable, while it will be found equally interesting and amusing by the casual reader. No tale has ever been written which has attained greater popularity or been more eagerly sought for while in the course of serial publication. The perusal of the introductory remarks will satisfy the reader that the Lawyer's Story contains incident of more than common interest.

SOME time ago, the following paragraph, copied from an English provincial newspaper, appeared in the New York *Sunday Dispatch*, and other journals of wide circulation :—

A MYSTERIOUS AFFAIR.—We find the following curious story in one of our English exchanges, and as it relates to a couple of Americans, we give it a place :— "The quiet little town of Hemmingford Abbotts, near St. Ives, Huntingtonshire, was recently visited by a young lady and gentleman from the United States, under circumstances that have created considerable excitement in the neighborhood. The parties are brother and sister, and we believe are contestants for the large property known as the Fitzherbert Manor Lands, situated in this county, which estates have for a long time been in dispute. As will be recollected, this property was formerly Crown Land, and was given by George the Fourth, when Prince Regent, to Herbert Fitzherbert, Esq., who subsequently went to America. The right of the Prince to bestow Crown Land was contested, and the estate thrown into chancery. Herbert Fitzherbert died, we believe, in the United States, and his heirs at law, after the decision of the long contested suit, entered into possession of the property. These heirs were a son and daughter. The arrival of the new contestants for this property created quite a stir among the fashionable circles. So far, however, but little has leaked out in reference to the real object of our trans-Atlantic visitors, who created the unusual stir in the locality above indicated. One of our reporters called at the Hotel at which the strangers stopped, to gather the particulars, if possible, but found the parties had taken their departure very mysteriously, no one at the hotel having the slightest intimation of their business or their present whereabouts. It is said, upon what authority we know not, that a distinguished attorney from London accompanied them, and that some parties were subpœnaed to attend a private examination, but failed to appear, and have not since been heard of by their friends. Altogether there appears to be considerable mystery about this affair."

Shortly afterwards, a letter was received by the editor of the *Dispatch* from a Retired member of the New York

Bar, who stated that he was perfectly acquainted with the history of the incident so mysteriously alluded to in the English journals, and who is the author of the narrative published by the title of the "Lawyer's Story," or the "Orphan's Wrongs."

Few narratives have surpassed the Lawyer's simple story in the intense interest it has excited. The attention of the reader is arrested immediately upon commencing the first chapter, and once having been commenced, the tale is read on with continually increasing interest to its conclusion.

The following is the letter alluded to, in which the author gives permission to the Editor of the *Dispatch* to publish the narrative:—

To the Editor of the ———.

SIR:—Noticing in the last number of the *Sunday Dispatch*, a paragraph copied from a Huntingtonshire (England) newspaper, headed a "Mysterious Affair," in which two Americans, brother and sister, are spoken of as playing a prominent part, I beg to inform you that I have had an intimate knowledge of the parties alluded to for the last ten years, and that I was the first person to cause an investigation to be made into their claims. For a short period also, I was professionally engaged in the case. I therefore can partially clear up the "Mystery" in which the matter, according to the reporter of the English paper, is involved. If you think proper I give you permission to publish the accompanying manuscript, containing the facts woven together in the form of a narrative. I have no interest in the matter; but as will be explained, my sympathies were from the first naturally enough enlisted in behalf of the American contestants, whose claims I considered indisputable, and I therefore watched every action *pro* and *con* that took place regarding their cause. Having retired from active practice, some six years since, I have made this case my hobby, and have but lately returned from Europe, where my services have voluntarily been rendered in behalf of the brother and sister. I am happy to say that the case has, after an arduous struggle, been decided in their favor, and that, so far as I know, they are now in secure and happy possession of the property it was sought to deprive them of. However, as I presume you will find the narrative to contain sufficient incident, and to possess sufficient interest to justify its publication, I will not anticipate the story. I give you my name in order to satisfy you that my statements are to be relied on; but it is not perhaps necessary that you should publish it, therefore I sign myself,

A Retired Member of the New York Bar.

February 6th, 1853.

www.ingramcontent.com/pod-product-compliance
Lightning Source LLC
LaVergne TN
LVHW010217110826
845151LV00004B/1116